Swedish Air Force guided missiles

Table of Contents

AGM-65 Maverick 1
AIM-120 AMRAAM 4
AIM-4 Falcon 10
AIM-9 Sidewinder 13
IRIS-T 21
RBS-15 23
RB 04 25
Rb 05 26
Skyflash 27

Preface

Each chapter in this book ends with a URL to a hyperlinked online version. Use the online version to access related pages, websites, footnotes, tables, color photos, updates, or to see the chapter's contributors. Click the edit link to suggest changes. Please type the URL exactly as it appears. If you change the URL's capitalization, for example, it may not work.

Purchase of this book entitles you to a free trial membership in the publisher's book club at www.booksllc.net. (Time limited offer.) Simply enter the barcode number from the back cover onto the membership form on our home page. The book club entitles you to select from millions of books at no additional charge, including a PDF copy of this and related books to read on the go. Simply enter the title or subject onto the search form to find them.

If you have any questions, could you please be so kind as to consult our Frequently Asked Questions page at www.booksllc.net/faqs.cfm? You are also welcome to contact us there.

Publisher: Books LLC, Wiki Series, Memphis, TN, USA, 2013.

AGM-65 Maverick

AGM-65 Maverick

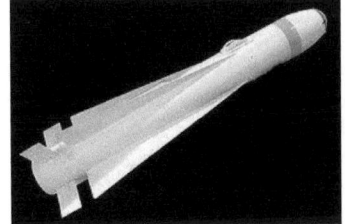

Type	Air-to-surface missile
Place of origin	United States
Service history	
In service	30 August 1972 – present
Used by	30+ countries
Wars	Vietnam War
	Yom Kippur War
	Iran–Iraq War
	Persian Gulf War
	Iraq War
	2011 Libyan civil war
Production history	
Manufacturer	Hughes Missile Systems; Raytheon
Unit cost	US$17,000 to $160,000, depending on variant
Number built	70,000+
Specifications	
Weight	462–670 lb (209–304 kg)
Length	8 feet 2 inches (2.49 m)
Diameter	12 in (30.5 cm)
Warhead	57 kg (125 lb) WDU-20/B charge (A/B/C models)
	136 kg (300 lb) WDU-24/B penetrating blast-fragmenta F/G/H/J/K models)
	E models utilize FMU-135/ delayed impact fuze
Engine	A/B:Thiokol SR109-TC-1
	D/E/F/G/H/J/K: SR114-TC Aerojet SR115-AJ-1) Solid propellant rocket motor via WPU-4/B or WPU-8/B pro section
Wingspan	2 ft 4 in (711 mm)
Propellant	Solid propellant
Operational range	Greater than 12 nmi (14 mi 22 km)
Speed	620 kn (715 mph or 1,150 k
Guidance system	Electro-optical in the A, B, and K models
	infrared imaging in the D, F G models
	laser in the E model
	charge-coupled device in H models

The **AGM-65 Maverick** is an air-to-ground tactical missile (AGM) designed for close air support. The most widely-produced precision-guided missile in the Western world, it is effective against a wide range of tactical targets, including armor, air defenses, ships, ground transportation and fuel storage facilities. Originally designed and built by Hughes Missile Systems, development of the AGM-65 spanned from 1966 to 1972, after which it entered service with the United States Air Force in August 1972. Since then, it has been exported to more than 30 countries and is certified on 25 aircraft. The Maverick served during the Vietnam, Yom Kippur, Iran–Iraq and Gulf Wars, along with other smaller conflicts, destroying enemy forces and installations with varying degrees of success.

Since its introduction into service, numerous Maverick versions had been designed and produced, using electro-optical, laser, charge-coupled device and infra-red guidance systems. The AGM-65 has two types of warhead: one has a contact fuze in the nose, the other has a heavyweight warhead fitted with a delayed-action fuze, which penetrates the target with its kinetic energy before detonating. The Maverick shares the same configuration as Hughes's AIM-4 Falcon and AIM-54 Phoenix, and measures more than 8 ft (2.4 m) in length and 12 in (30 cm) in diameter.

Development

The Maverick's development history began in 1965, when the United States Air Force (USAF) began a program to develop a replacement to the AGM-12 Bullpup. With a range of 8.8 nm (14.8 km), the radio-guided Bullpup was introduced in 1959 and was considered a "silver bullet" by operators. However, the launch aircraft was required to fly straight towards the target during the missile's flight instead of performing evasive manoeuvres, thus placing the crew in significant risks.

From 1966 to 1968, Hughes Missile Systems and Rockwell competed for the contract to build the new missile. Each were allocated $3 million for preliminary design and engineering of the Maverick in 1966. In 1968, Hughes emerged with the $95 million contract for further development and testing of the missile; at the same time, contract options called for 17,000 missiles to be procured. Hughes conducted a smooth development of the AGM-65 Maverick, culminating in the first, and successful, firing of the AGM-65 on a tank at Air Force Missile Development Center at Holloman Air Force Base, New Mexico, on 18 December 1969. In July 1971, the USAF and Hughes signed a $69.9 million contract for 2,000 missiles, the first of which was delivered in 1972.

Although early operational results were favorable, military planners predicted that the Maverick would fare less successfully in the hazy conditions in Central Europe, where it would have been used against Warsaw Pact forces. As such, development of the AGM-65B began in 1975 before it was delivered during the late 1970s. When production of the AGM-65A/B was ended in 1978, more than 35,000 Mavericks had been built.

More versions of the Maverick appeared, among which was laser-guided AGM-65C/E. Development of the AGM-65C started in 1978 by Rockwell, who built a number of development missiles for the USAF. Due to high cost, the version was not procured by the USAF, and instead entered service with the United States Marine Corps (USMC) as

An AGM-65 test-fired against an M-48 tank (1978)

the AGM-65E. Another major development was the AGM-65D, which employed an imaging infrared (IIR) seeker and thus is all-weather operable. The five-year development period of the AGM-65D started in 1977 and ended with the first delivery to the USAF in October 1983. The version received initial operating capability in February 1986.

The AGM-65F is a hybrid Maverick combining the AGM-65D's IIR seeker and warhead and propulsion components of the AGM-65E. Deployed by the United States Navy (USN), the AGM-65F is optimized for maritime strike roles. The first AGM-65F launch from the P-3C took place in 1989, and in 1994, the USN awarded Unisys a contract to integrate the version with the P-3C. Meanwhile, Hughes produced the AGM-65G, which essentially has the same guidance system as the D, with some software modifications that track larger targets, coupled with a shaped-charge warhead.

In the mid-1990s to early 2000s, there were several ideas of enhancing the Maverick's potential. Among them was the stillborn plan to incorporate to Mavericks active millimeter wave radars, which can determine the exact shape of a target. Another study called "Longhorn Project" was conducted by Hughes, and later Raytheon following the absorption of Hughes into Raytheon, looked a Maverick version equipped with turbojet engines instead of rocket motors. The "Maverick ER", as it was dubbed, would have a "significant increase in range" compared to the Maverick's current range of 16 miles (25 km). The proposal was abandoned, but if the Maverick ER had entered production, it would have replaced the AGM-119B Penguin carried on the MH-60R.

The most modern versions of the Maverick are the AGM-65H/K, which were in production as of 2007. The AGM-65H was developed by taking coupling the AGM-56B with a charge-coupled device (CCD) seeker optimized for desert operations and which has three times the range of the original TV-sensor; a parallel USN program aimed at rebuilding AGM-65Fs with newer CCD seekers resulted in the AGM-65J. The AGM-65K, meanwhile, was developed by replacing the AGM-65G's IR guidance system with an electro-optical television guidance system.

Design

The Maverick has a modular design construction, allowing different combination of the guidance package and warhead to be attached to the rocket motor section to produce a different weapon. It has long-chord delta wings and a cylindrical body, reminiscent of the AIM-4 Falcon and the AIM-54 Phoenix.

Different models of the AGM-65 have used electro-optical, laser, and infra-red guidance systems. The AGM-65 has two types of warheads: one has a contact fuze in the nose, the other has a heavyweight warhead fitted with a delayed-action fuze, which penetrates the target with its kinetic energy before detonating. The latter is most effective against large, hard targets. The propulsion system for both types is a solid-fuel rocket motor behind the warhead.

The Maverick missile is unable to

lock onto targets on its own; it has to be given input by the pilot or Weapon Systems Officer (WSO) after which it follows the path to the target autonomously, allowing the WSO to fire and forget. In an A-10, for example, the video fed from the seeker head is relayed to a screen in the cockpit, where the pilot can check the locked target of the missile before launch. A crosshair on the head-up display is shifted by the pilot to set the approximate target while the missile will then automatically recognize and lock on to the target. Once the missile is launched, it requires no further assistance from the launch vehicle and tracks its target automatically. This fire-and-forget property is not shared by the E version that uses semi-active laser homing.

Variants

Laser AGM-65 Maverick on a USN F/A-18C, 2004.

Maverick A is the basic model and uses an electro-optical television guidance system. No longer in U.S. service.
Maverick B is similar to the A model, although the B model added optical zooming to lock onto small or distant targets.
Maverick C was to be a laser-guided variant for the United States Marine Corps (USMC). It was canceled before production, however its requirement was later met by the Maverick E.
Maverick D replaced the electro-optical guidance with an imaging infrared system which doubled practical firing distance and allowed for use at night and during bad weather. A reduced smoke rocket engine was also introduced in this model. Achieved initial operation capability in 1983.
Maverick E uses a laser designator guidance system optimized for fortified installations and heavier penetrating blast-fragmentation warhead (300 lb or 140 kg vs. 125 lb or 57 kg in older models). Achieved IOC in 1985 and used mainly by USMC aviation.
Maverick F, designed specially for US Navy, uses a modified Maverick D infrared guidance system optimized for tracking ships fitted onto Maverick-E body and warhead.
Maverick G model essentially has the same guidance system as the D with some software modification that enables the pilot to track larger targets. The G model's major difference is its heavier penetrator warhead taken from Maverick E, compared to the D model's shaped-charge warhead. Completed tests in 1988.
Maverick H model is an AGM-65B/D missile upgraded with a new charge-coupled device (CCD) seeker better suited for desert environment.
Maverick J model is a Navy AGM-65F missile upgraded with the new CCD seeker. However this conversion is not confirmed.
Maverick K model is an AGM-65G upgraded with the CCD seeker, at least 1200, but possibly up to 2500, AGM-65G rounds are planned for conversion to AGM-65K standard.
Maverick L model incorporates a laser-guided seeker.

Deployment

The Maverick was declared operational on 30 August 1972 with the F-4D/Es and A-7s initially cleared for the type; the missile made its combat debut four months later with the USAF in the Vietnam War. During the Yom Kippur War in October 1973, the Israelis used Mavericks to destroy and disable enemy vehicles. Deployment of early versions of the Mavericks in these two wars were successful due to the favorable atmospheric conditions that suited the electro-optical TV seeker. Ninety-nine missiles were fired during the two wars, eighty-four of which were successful.

In June 1975, during a border confrontation, Iranian troops fired twelve Mavericks, all successful, at Iraqi tanks. Five years later, during Operation Morvarid as part of the Iran–Iraq War, Iranian F-4s used Mavericks to sink three OSA IIs and four P-6s combat ships.

In August 1990, Iraq invaded Kuwait. In early 1991, the U.S.-led Coalition executed Operation Desert Storm during which Mavericks played a crucial role in the ousting of Iraqi forces from Kuwait. Employed by F-15Es, F-18, AV-8Bs, F-16s and A-10s, but used mainly by the last two, more than 5,000 Mavericks were deployed to attack armored targets. The most-used variant by the USAF was the IIR-guided AGM-65D. The reported hit rate by USAF Mavericks was 80–90 percent, while for the USMC it was 60 percent. The Maverick was again used in Iraq during the 2003 Iraq War, during which 918 were fired.

The first time the Maverick were fired from a Lockheed P-3 Orion at a hostile vessel was when the USN and coalition units came to aid of Libyan rebels to engage Libyan Coast Guard vessel *Vittoria* in the port of Misrata, Libya, during the late evening of 28 March 2011. *Vittoria* was engaged and fired upon by a USN P-3C Maritime Patrol aircraft with AGM-65 Maverick missiles. Iranian AGM-65 Maverick missiles have been used in various operations such as Fatholmobin whereas Iranian AH-1J's fired 11 Mavericks.

Launch platforms

US Navy F/A-18C Hornet armed with AGM-65 Maverick

United States

LAU-117 Maverick launchers have

An IRIAF F-4E Phantom II carrying four AGM-65 Maverick

been used on USN, USAF, and USMC aircraft:
Bell AH-1W SuperCobra
Boeing AH-64 Apache
Boeing F/A-18E/F Super Hornet
Douglas A-4M Skyhawk
Grumman A-6 Intruder
Fairchild Republic A-10 Thunderbolt II
General Dynamics F-111 Aardvark
General Dynamics F-16 Fighting Falcon
Kaman SH-2G Seasprite
Lockheed P-3 Orion
LTV A-7 Corsair II
McDonnell Douglas AV-8B Harrier II
McDonnell Douglas F-4 Phantom II
McDonnell Douglas F-15E Strike Eagle
McDonnell Douglas F/A-18 Hornet

Export

The Maverick has been exported to at least 30 countries:

Royal Australian Air Force: F/A-18
Belgian Air Component: F-16 (AGM-65G)
Royal Canadian Air Force: CF-18
Chilean Air Force: F-16 AM/BM MLU, F-16 Block 50+
Czech Air Force: L-159
Royal Danish Air Force: F-16
Egyptian Air Force: F-4 and F-16 (AGM-65A/B/E)
Hellenic Air Force: F-4 and F-16 Blocks 30, 50, and 52+
Hungarian Air Force: JAS 39
Indonesian Air Force: F-16A/B Block 15 OCU, Hawk 209
Islamic Republic of Iran Air Force: F-4E and SH-3D
Israeli Air Force: F-4E and F-16
Italian Navy: AV-8B
Royal Jordanian Air Force: F-16 MLU and F-5E/F
Kuwait Air Force.
Royal Malaysian Air Force: F/A-18D, and Hawk 208
Royal Moroccan Air Force: F-16 Block 52+, F-5E/F
Royal Netherlands Air Force: F-16 MLU
Royal New Zealand Navy: SH-2G; and Royal New Zealand Air Force: A-4 (after being upgraded in the late 1980s under Project Kahu, retired 2001)
Pakistan Air Force: F-16
Polish Air Force: F-16 Block 50/52+
Portuguese Air Force: F-16A/B Block 15 OCU and F-16AM/BM MLU
Royal Saudi Air Force: F-5E
Serbian Air Force: J-22 and G-4
Republic of Singapore Air Force: A-4SU, F-5S, F-16C/D Block 52 and F-15SG
Republic of Korea Air Force: A-50, F-16C/D Block 52D, F-15K, F-4
Spanish Air Force: F/A-18; and Spanish Navy: AV-8B
Swedish Air Force: AJ37 JAS 39
Swiss Air Force: F-5E and Hunter
Republic of China Air Force (Taiwan): F-16A/B Block 20 (AGM-65G), F-CK-1 and F-5E/F (AGM-65B)
Royal Thai Air Force: F-16A/B Block 15 OCU/ADF and JAS 39
Turkish Air Force: F-16 and F-4
Royal Air Force: Harrier GR7
JASDF: F-1, F-2 and F-4
Source http://en.wikipedia.org/wiki/AGM-65_Maverick

AIM-120 AMRAAM

AIM-120 AMRAAM

An AIM-120 AMRAAM mounted on the wingtip launcher of an F-16 Fighting Falcon fighter plane

Type	Medium-range, active radar homing air-to-air missile
Place of origin	United States
Service history	
In service	September 1991–present
Used by	See *operators*
Production history	
Manufacturer	• Hughes: 1991-1997
	• Raytheon: 1997-present
Unit cost	• $300–$400,000 for 120C variants
	• $1,470,000 for 120D (201
Variants	AIM-120A, AIM-120B, AI 120C, AIM-120C-4/5/6/7, 120D
Specifications	
Weight	335 pounds (152 kg)
Length	12 feet (3.7 m)
Diameter	7 inches (180 mm)
Warhead	High explosive blast-fragmentation
	• AIM-120A/B: WDU-33/E pounds (22.7 kg)
	• AIM-120C-5: WDU-41/B pounds (18.1 kg)
Detonation mechanism	Active RADAR Target Detection Device (TDD)
	Quadrant Target Detection Device (QTDD) in AIM-12 6 – Lots 13 and up.

Engine	solid-fuel rocket motor
Wingspan	20.7 inches (530 mm) (AIM 120A/B)
Operational range	• AIM-120A/B 55–75 km (40 nm)
	• AIM-120C-5 >105 km (> nm)
	• AIM-120D (C-8) >180 kr (>97 nm)
Speed	Mach 4
Guidance system	INS, active radar
Launch platform	Aircraft: AV-8B+ Harrier II BAE Sea Harrier Eurofighter Typhoon F-4 Phantom II Grumman F-14 Tomcat McDonnell Douglas F-1 Eagle McDonnell Douglas F-1 Strike Eagle General Dynamics F-16 Fighting Falcon F/A-18 Hornet F/A-18E/F Super Horne F-22 Raptor F-5S/T Panavia Tornado ADV JA 37 Viggen Saab JAS 39 Gripen **Surface-launched:** NASAMS and others

The **AIM-120 Advanced Medium-Range Air-to-Air Missile**, or **AMRAAM** (pronounced "am-ram"), is a modern beyond-visual-range air-to-air missile (BVRAAM) capable of all-weather day-and-night operations. Designed with the same form-and-fit factors as the previous generation of semi-active guided Sparrow missiles, it is a fire-and-forget missile with active guidance. When an AMRAAM missile is being launched, NATO pilots use the brevity code - **Fox Three**.

Origins

AIM-7 Sparrow MRM

The AIM-7 Sparrow medium range missile (MRM) was purchased by the US Navy from original developer Howard Hughes in the 1950s as its first operational air-to-air missile with "beyond visual range" (BVR) capability. With an effective range of about 12 miles (19 km), it was introduced as a radar beam riding missile and then it was improved to a semiactive radar guided missile which would home in on reflections from a target illuminated by the radar of the launching aircraft. It was effective at visual to beyond visual range. The early beam riding versions of the Sparrow missiles were integrated onto the F3H Demon and F7U Cutlass, but the definitive AIM-7 Sparrow was the primary weapon for the all-weather F-4 Phantom II fighter/interceptor, which lacked an internal gun in its early U.S. Navy, U.S. Marine Corps, and early U.S. Air Force versions. The F-4 carried up to four AIM-7s in built-in recesses under its belly.

Although designed for non-maneuvering targets such as bombers, due to poor performance against fighters over North Vietnam, these missiles were progressively improved until they proved highly effective in dogfights. Together with the short range infrared guided AIM-9 Sidewinder, they replaced the AIM-4 Falcon IR and radar guided series for use in air combat by the USAF as well. A disadvantage to semiactive homing was that only one target could be illuminated by the launching fighter plane at a time. Also, the launching aircraft had to remain pointed in the direction of the target (within the azimuth and elevation of its own radar set) which could be difficult or dangerous in air-to-air combat.

AIM-54 Phoenix LRM

The US Navy later developed the AIM-54 Phoenix long range missile (LRM) for the fleet air defense mission. It was a large 1,000 lb (500 kg) Mach 4 missile designed to counter cruise missiles and the bombers that launched them. Originally intended for the straight-wing F6D Missileer and then the navalized version of the F-111B, it finally saw service with the Grumman F-14 Tomcat, the only fighter capable of carrying such a heavy missile. Phoenix was the first US fire-and-forget multiple launch radar-guided missile: one which used its own active guidance system to guide itself without help from the launch aircraft when it closed on its target. This in theory gave a Tomcat with a six-Phoenix load the unprecedented capability of tracking and destroying up to six targets beyond visual range, as far as 100 miles (160 km) away – the only US fighter with such capability.

A full load of six Phoenix missiles and its 2,000 pounds (910 kg) dedicated launcher exceeded a typical Vietnam-era bomb load; only one, two or four missiles were normally flown off the carrier, as a full load was too heavy for a carrier landing. Although highly lauded in the press, its service in the US Navy was primarily as a deterrent, as its use was hampered by restrictive Rules of engagement in conflicts such as Operations Desert Storm, Southern Watch and Iraqi Freedom. The only reported combat successes were by Iranian Tomcats against Iraqi opponents. The US Navy retired the Phoenix in 2004 in light of availability of the AIM-120 AMRAAM on the F/A-18 Hornet and the pending retirement of the F-14 Tomcat from active service in late 2006.

ACEVAL/AIMVAL

The Department of Defense conducted an extensive evaluation of air combat tactics and missile technology from 1974-78 at Nellis AFB using the F-14 Tomcat and F-15 Eagle equipped with Sparrow and Sidewinder missiles as blue force and Aggressor F-5E aircraft equipped with AIM-9L all-aspect Sidewinders as the Red force. This Joint Test and Evaluaton (JT&E) was designated Air Combat Evaluation / Air Intercept Missile Evaluation (ACEVAL/AIMVAL). A principal finding was the necessity to produce illumination for the Sparrow until impact resulted in the Red Force being able to launch their all-aspect Sidewinders before impact thereby resulting in mutual kills. What was needed was Phoenix type multiple launch and terminal active capability in a Sparrow size airframe. This led to a Memorandum of Agreement (MOA) with European allies (principally the UK and Germany for development) for the US to develop an Advanced Medium Range Air-to-Air Missile (AMRAAM) with the USAF as lead service. The MOA also assigned responsibility for development of an Advanced Short Range Air-to-Air Missile to the European team - this would become the British ASRAAM.

Requirements

Surface-to-air mounting (shown: CATM-120C captive training variant)

By the 1990s, the reliability of the Sparrow had improved so much from the dismal days of Vietnam that it accounted for the largest number of aerial targets destroyed in Desert Storm. But while the USAF had passed on the Phoenix and their own similar AIM-47/YF-12 to optimize dogfight performance, they still needed a multiple-launch fire-and-forget capability for the F-15 and F-16. AMRAAM would need to be fitted on fighters as small as the F-16, and fit in the same spaces that were designed to fit the Sparrow on the F-4 Phantom. The European partners needed AMRAAM to be integrated on aircraft as small as the Sea Harrier. The US Navy needed AMRAAM to be carried on the F/A-18 Hornet and wanted capability for two to be carried on a launcher that normally carried one Sparrow to allow for more air-to-ground weapons.

The AMRAAM became one of the primary air-to-air weapons of the new F-22 Raptor fighter, which needed to place all of its weapons into internal weapons bays in order to help achieve an extremely low radar cross-section. The U.S. Navy also needed to retire its old and worn out F-14 Tomcats, and then pass its Fleet Air Defense mission on to newer fighter planes: the F/A-18C/D Hornets and F/A-18E/F Super Hornets with medium-range air-to-air missiles. Also, the combat threats to the Navy's aircraft carrier task forces had changed dramatically following the collapse of the Soviet Union and its powerful navy and air force.

Development

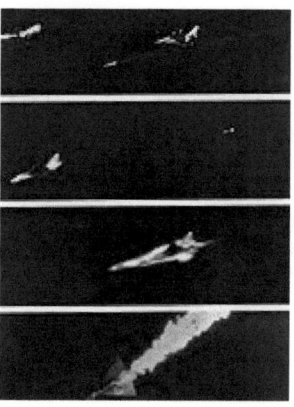

First successful test at the White Sands Missile Range, New Mexico 1982

AMRAAM was developed as the result of an agreement (the Family of Weapons MOA, no longer in effect by 1990), among the United States and several other NATO nations to develop air-to-air missiles and to share production technology. Under this agreement the U.S. was to develop the next generation medium range missile (AMRAAM) and Europe would develop the next generation short range missile (ASRAAM). When the German ASRAAM seeker development ran into problems, the MOA was abrogated and this breakdown led to the U.S. developing AIM-9X Sidewinder and Germany the IRIS-T. Although Europe initially adopted the AMRAAM, an effort to develop the MBDA Meteor, a competitor to AMRAAM, was begun in Great Britain. Eventually the ASRAAM was developed solely by the British, but using another source for its infrared seeker. After protracted development, the deployment of AMRAAM (AIM-120A) began in September 1991 in U.S. Air Force F-15 Eagle fighter squadrons. The U.S. Navy soon followed (in 1993) in its the F/A-18 Hornet squadrons.

The eastern counterpart of AMRAAM is the somewhat similar Russian Air Force AA-12 "Adder", sometimes called in the West as the "AMRAAMski." Likewise, France began its own air-to-air missile development with the MICA concept that used a common airframe for separate radar-guided and infrared-guided versions.

Operational features summary

AMRAAM has an all-weather, beyond-visual-range (BVR) capability. It improves the aerial combat capabilities of U.S. and allied aircraft to meet the current threat of enemy air-to-air weapons as they existed in 1991. AMRAAM serves as a follow-on to the AIM-7 Sparrow missile series. The new missile is faster, smaller, and lighter, and has improved capabilities against low-altitude targets. It also incorporates a datalink to guide the missile to a point where its active radar turns on and makes terminal intercept of the target. An inertial reference unit and microcomputer system makes the missile less dependent upon the fire-control system of the aircraft.

Once the missile closes in on the target, its active radar guides it to intercept. This feature, known as "fire-and-forget", frees the aircrew from the need to further provide guidance, enabling the aircrew to aim and fire several missiles simultaneously at multiple targets and perform evasive maneuvers while the missiles guide themselves to the targets.

The missile also features the ability to "Home on Jamming," giving it the ability to switch over from active radar homing to passive homing – homing on jamming signals from the target aircraft. Software on board the missile allows it to detect if it is being jammed, and guide on its target using the proper guidance system.

Guidance system overview

Interception course stage

AMRAAM uses two-stage guidance when fired at long range. The aircraft passes data to the missile just before

Grumman F-14 Tomcat carrying an AMRAAM during a 1982 test

launch, giving it information about the location of the target aircraft from the launch point and its direction and speed. The missile uses this information to fly on an interception course to the target using its built in inertial navigation system (INS). This information is generally obtained using the launching aircraft's radar, although it could come from an infrared search and tracking system (IRST), from a data link from another fighter aircraft, or from an AWACS aircraft.

After launch, If the firing aircraft or surrogate continues to track the target, periodic updates—such as changes in the target's direction and speed—are sent from the launch aircraft to the missile, allowing the missile to adjust its course so that it is able to close to a self-homing distance where it will be close enough to "catch" the target aircraft in the *basket* (the missile's radar field of view in which it will be able to lock onto the target aircraft, unassisted by the launch aircraft).

Not all armed services using the AMRAAM have elected to purchase the mid-course update option, which limits AMRAAM's effectiveness in some scenarios. The RAF initially opted not to use mid-course update for its Tornado F3 force, only to discover that without it, testing proved the AMRAAM was less effective in BVR engagements than the older semiactive radar homing BAE Skyflash weapon—the AIM-120's own radar is necessarily of limited range and power compared to that of the launch aircraft.

Terminal stage and impact

Once the missile closes to self-homing distance, it turns on its active radar seeker and searches for the target aircraft. If the target is in or near the expected location, the missile will find it and guide itself to the target from this point. At the point where an AMRAAM switches to autonomous self-guidance, the NATO "Husky" or "Pitbull" would be called out on the radio, just as "Fox Three" would be called out upon launch.

If the missile is fired at short range (typically visual range), it can use its active seeker just after launch, making the missile truly "fire and forget". The NATO brevity code "Fox 3 close" is used in this situation (the pilot can say only Fox 3, but he can add a distance information: "long" for maximum range shot, "medium" for medium ranges (around 15 nm) and close for within visual range (WVR) shot. However, this tactic is considerably risky – the now-active AMRAAM will acquire and home in on the first target it sees, regardless of friend or foe.

Boresight mode

Apart from the slave mode, there is a free guidance mode, called boresight. This mode is radar guidance-free, the missile just fires and locks the first thing it sees. When this mode is selected, the HUD displays a circle which represent "sight" of the missile. When the pilot fires, he says "Maddog". This mode can be used for defensive shot, i.e. when the enemy has numerical superiority.

Kill probability and tactics

General considerations

The kill probability (P) is determined by several factors, including aspect (head-on interception, side-on or tail-chase), altitude, the speed of the missile and the target, and how hard the target can turn. Typically, if the missile has sufficient energy during the terminal phase, which comes from being launched at close range to the target from an aircraft with an altitude and speed advantage, it will have a good chance of success. This chance drops as the missile is fired at longer ranges as it runs out of overtake speed at long ranges, and if the target can force the missile to turn it might bleed off enough speed that it can no longer chase the target. Operationally, the missile, which was designed for beyond visual range combat, has a P of 46% when fired at targets beyond visual range (13 missiles for 6 kills). In addition, the targets lacked missile warning systems, were not maneuvering, and were not attempting to engage the fighter that fired the AMRAAM. One of the targets was a US Army Blackhawk helicopter.

Lower-capability targets

This leads to two main engagement scenarios. If the target is not armed with any medium or long-range fire-and-forget weapons, the attacking aircraft need only get close enough to the target and launch the AMRAAM. In these scenarios, the AMRAAM has a high chance of hitting, especially against low-maneuverability targets. The launch distance depends upon whether the target is heading towards or away from the firing aircraft. In a head-on engagement, the missile can be launched at longer range, since the range will be closing fast. In this situation, even if the target turns around, it is unlikely it can speed up and fly away fast enough to avoid being overtaken and hit by the missile (as long as the missile is not released too early). It is also unlikely the enemy can outmaneuver the missile since the closure rate will be so great. In a tail-on engagement, the firing aircraft might have to close to between one-half and one-quarter maximum range (or maybe even closer for a very fast target) in order to give the missile sufficient energy to overtake the targets.

If the targets are armed with missiles, the fire-and-forget nature of the AMRAAM is valuable, enabling the launching aircraft to fire missiles at the target and subsequently take defensive actions. Even if the targets have longer-range semiactive radar homing (SARH) missiles, they will have to chase the launching aircraft in order for the missiles to track them, effectively flying right into the AMRAAM. If the target aircraft fires missiles and then turns and runs away, those missiles will not be able to hit. Of course, if the target aircraft have long range missiles, even if they are not fire-and-forget, the fact that they force the launching aircraft to turn and run reduces the kill probability, since it is possible that without the mid-course updates the missiles will not find the target aircraft. However the chance of success is still good and compared to the relative impunity the launching aircraft enjoy, this gives the AMRAAM-equipped aircraft a decisive edge. If one or more missiles fail to hit, the AMRAAM-equipped aircraft can turn and re-engage, although they will be at a disadvantage compared to the chasing aircraft due to the speed they lose in the turn, and would have to be careful that they are not being tracked with SARH missiles.

Similarly armed targets

The other main engagement scenario is against other aircraft with fire-and-forget missiles like the Vympel R-77 (NATO AA-12 "Adder") — perhaps MiG-29s, Su-27s or similar. In this case engagement is very much down to teamwork and could be described as "a game of chicken." Both flights of aircraft can fire their missiles at each other beyond visual range (BVR), but then face the problem that if they continue to track the target aircraft in order to provide mid-course updates for the missile's flight, they are also flying into their opponents' missiles. This assumes of course that all aircraft will detect each other.

Variants and upgrades

An AIM-120 AMRAAM missile on display at the U.S. National Air and Space Museum

Air-to-air missile versions

There are currently four main variants of AMRAAM, all in service with the

AIM-120 AMRAAM (right) fitted in a weapons bay of a F-22 Raptor

United States Air Force, USN, and the United States Marine Corps. The **AIM-120A** is no longer in production and shares the enlarged wings and fins with the successor **AIM-120B**. The AIM-120C has smaller "clipped" aerosurfaces to enable internal carriage on the USAF F-22 Raptor. AIM-120B deliveries began in 1994.

The **AIM-120C** deliveries began in 1996. The C-variant has been steadily upgraded since it was introduced. The AIM-120C-6 contained an improved fuse (Target Detection Device) compared to its predecessor. The AIM-120C-7 development began in 1998 and included improvements in homing and greater range (actual amount of improvement unspecified). It was successfully tested in 2003 and is currently being produced for both domestic and foreign customers. It helped the U.S. Navy replace the F-14 Tomcats with F/A-18E/F Super Hornets – the loss of the F-14's long-range AIM-54 Phoenix missiles (already retired) is offset with a longer-range AMRAAM-D. The lighter weight of the advanced AMRAAM enables a hornet pilot greater bring-back weight upon carrier landings.

The **AIM-120D** is an upgraded version of the AMRAAM with improvements in almost all areas, including 50% greater range (than the already-extended range AIM-120C-7) and better guidance over its entire flight envelope yielding an improved kill probability (P). Raytheon began testing the D model on 5 August 2008, the company reported that an AIM-120D launched from an F/A-18F Super Hornet passed within lethal distance of a QF-4 target drone at the White Sands Missile Range.

The AIM-120D (P3I Phase 4, formerly known as AIM-120C-8) is a development of the AIM-120C with a two-way data link, more accurate navigation using a GPS-enhanced IMU, an expanded no-escape envelope, improved HOBS (High-Angle Off-Boresight) capability, and a 50% increase in range. The AIM-120D is a joint USAF/USN project, and is currently in the testing phase.

There are also plans for Raytheon to develop a ramjet-powered derivative of the AMRAAM, the Future Medium Range Air-Air Missile (FMRAAM). It is not known whether the FMRAAM will be produced since the target market, the British Ministry of Defence, has chosen the Meteor missile over the FMRAAM for a BVR missile for the Eurofighter Typhoon aircraft.

Raytheon is also working with the Missile Defense Agency to develop the Network Centric Airborne Defense Element (NCADE), an anti-ballistic missile derived from the AIM-120. This weapon will be equipped with a Ramjet engine and an IR seeker derived from the Sidewinder missile. In place of a proximity-fused warhead, the NCADE will use a kinetic energy hit-to-kill vehicle based on the one used in the Navy's RIM-161 Standard Missile 3.

The −120A and −120B models are currently nearing the end of their service life while the −120D variant has just entered full production. AMRAAM was due to be replaced by the USAF, the U.S. Navy, and the U.S. Marine Corps after 2020 by the Joint Dual Role Air Dominance Missile (JDRADM). This was unexpectedly terminated in the 2013 budget plan, and so the future replacement is uncertain.

Ground-launched systems

Raytheon successfully tested launching AMRAAM missiles from a five-missile carrier on a M1097 Humvee. This system will be known as the **SLAM-RAAM** (Surface Launched (SL) and AMRAAM). They receive their initial guidance information from a radar not mounted on the vehicle. Since the mis-

Battery of four SL-AMRAAM on HMMWV

sile is launched without the benefit of an aircraft's speed or high altitude, its range is considerably shorter. Raytheon is currently marketing an SL-AMRAAM EX, purported to be an extended range AMRAAM and bearing a resemblance to the ESSM (Evolved Sea Sparrow Missile).

The Norwegian Advanced Surface-to-Air Missile System (NASAMS), developed by Kongsberg Defence & Aerospace, consists of a number of vehicle-pulled launch batteries (containing six AMRAAMs each) along with separate radar trucks and control station vehicles.

While still under evaluation for replacement of current US Army assets, the SL-AMRAAM has been deployed in several nations military forces. The United Arab Emirates (UAE) has requested the purchasing of SL-AMRAAM as part of a larger 7 billion dollar foreign military sales package. The sale would include 288 AMRAAM C-7 missiles.

The US Army has test fired the SL-AMRAAM from a HIMARS artillery rocket launcher as a common launcher, as part of a move to switch to a larger and more survivable launch platform.

The National Guard Association of the United States has sent a letter asking for the United States Senate to stop the Army's plan to drop the SLAMRAAM program because without it there would be no path to modernize the Guard's AN/TWQ-1 Avenger Battalions.

On 6 January 2011, Secretary of Defense Robert M. Gates announced that the U.S. Army has decided to terminate acquisition of the SLAMRAAM as part of a budget-cutting effort.

Operational history

The AMRAAM was used for the first time on 27 December 1992, when a USAF F-16D shot down an Iraqi MiG-25 that violated the southern no-fly-zone. Interestingly enough, this missile was returned from the flight line as defective a day earlier. AMRAAM gained a second victory in January 1993 when an Iraqi MiG-23 was shot down by a USAF F-16C.

The third combat use of the AMRAAM was in 1994, when a Republika Srpska Air Force J-21 Jastreb aircraft was shot down by a USAF F-16C that was patrolling the UN-imposed no-fly-zone over Bosnia. In that engagement at least 3 other Serbian aircraft were shot down by USAF F-16C fighters using AIM-9 missiles (see Banja Luka incident for more details). At that point three launches in combat resulted in three kills, resulting in the AMRAAM being informally named "slammer" in the second half of the 1990s.

In 1998 and 1999 AMRAAMs were again fired by USAF F-15 fighters at Iraqi aircraft violating the No-Fly-Zone, but this time they failed to hit their targets. During the spring of 1999, AMRAAMs saw their main combat action during Operation Allied Force, the Kosovo bombing campaign. Six Serbian MiG-29 were shot down by NATO (4 USAF F-15C, 1 USAF F-16C, 1 Dutch F-16A MLU), all of them using AIM-120 missiles (the kill by the F-16C may have happened due to friendly fire, from SA-7 MANPAD fired by Serbian infantry).

As of mid 2008, the AIM-120 AMRAAM has shot down nine aircraft (six MiG-29s, one MiG-25, one MiG-23, and one Soko J-21 Jastreb). An AMRAAM was also involved in a friendly-fire incident in 1994 when F-15 fighters patrolling the Northern No-Fly Zone inadvertently shot down a pair of U.S. Army Black Hawk helicopters.

Since 2007 Raytheon has continued to slip on AMRAAM deliveries, leading the USAF to withhold $621 million in 2012 on account of 193 missiles not delivered.

Foreign sales

In 2006 Poland received AIM-120C-5 missiles to arm its new F-16C/D Block 52+ fighters.

In early 2006 the Pakistan Air Force (PAF) ordered 500 AIM-120C-5 AMRAAM missiles as part of a $650 million F-16 ammunition deal to equip the PAF's F-16C/D Block 52+ and F-16A/B MLU fighters. The PAF get the first three F-16 Block 52+ on 3 July 2010 and first batch of AMRAAMs on 26 July 2010.

In 2007, the United States government agreed to sell 218 AIM-120C-7 missiles to Taiwan as part of a large arms sales package that also included 235 AGM-65G-2 Maverick missiles. Total value of the package, including launchers, maintenance, spare parts, support and training rounds, was estimated at around $421 million USD. This supplemented an earlier Taiwanese purchase of 120 AIM-120C-5 missiles a few years ago.

2008 has brought announcements of new or additional sales to Singapore, Finland, Morocco and South Korea; in December 2010 the Swiss government requested 150 AIM-120C-7 missiles. Sales to Finland have stalled, because the manufacturer has not been able to fix a mysterious bug that causes the rocket motors of the missile to fail in cold tests.

Mysterious Cold Weather Malfunction

Finnish Defence Forces reported on 3 September 2012 that the United States had not delivered any of the AMRAAM anti-aircraft missiles they had ordered due to a mysterious engine malfunction in cold weather that the manufacturer, Raytheon, has not been able to determine the fault of. Colonel Kari Renko, an engineer at the Finnish Air Force, was quoted by Helsingin Sanomat as saying about this failure, *"The problem involves the rocket engines which have been in use for decades"* and that Finland first was told of the problems by the Americans about two years ago. The reason for the malfunction has been determined to be a change in the chemical formula of the rocket propellant to comply with new environmental regulations. The change caused the supplier of AMRAAM rocket motors, Alliant Techsystems, to produce motors that were unreliable, especially in cold conditions where aircraft carrying them would fly. ATK has been unable to find a solution, and no new AMRAAM missiles had been delivered to the USAF since 2010 as a result. In late 2012, the Air Force solved the problem by selecting Norwegian ammunition manufacturer Nammo to be their new supplier of AMRAAM rocket motors.

Operators

Australia
Royal Australian Air Force
F/A-18A/B Hornet
F/A-18F Super Hornet

Belgium
Belgian Air Component
F-16 Fighting Falcon

Bahrain
Royal Bahraini Air Force
F-16 Fighting Falcon

Canada
Royal Canadian Air Force
CF-188

Japan
Japan Air Self-Defense Force
F-15J Eagle Mitsubishi F-2

Jordan
Royal Jordanian Air Force
F-16 Fighting Falcon

Kuwait
Kuwait Air Force
F/A-18C/D Hornet

Morocco
Royal Moroccan Air Force
F-16 Fighting Falcon

Royal Malaysian Air Force
Northrop

South Korea
Republic of Korea Air Force
F-15K Slam Eagle
F-16 Fighting Falcon

Switzerland
Swiss Air Force
F/A-18C/D Hornet

Spain
Spanish Air Force
F/A-18 Hornet
Eurofighter Typhoon
Spanish Army NASAMS
Spanish Navy AV-8 Harrier II

Chile
Chilean Air Force
F-16 Fighting Falcon

Czech Republic
Czech Air Force
Saab JAS 39 Gripen

Denmark
Danish Air Force
F-16 Fighting Falcon

Finland
Finnish Air Force
F/A-18 Hornet
NASAMS 2 (ordered)

Germany
German Air Force
F-4 Phantom II
Eurofighter Typhoon

Greece
Hellenic Air Force
F-4 Phantom II
F-16 Fighting Falcon

Hungary
Hungarian Air Force
Saab JAS

RF-5
F/A-18D Hornet

Netherlands
Royal Netherlands Air Force
F-16 Fighting Falcon
Royal Netherlands Army NASAMS

Norway
Royal Norwegian Air Force
F-16 Fighting Falcon
F-CK-1 Northrop F-5E/F

Oman
Royal Air Force of Oman (RAFO)
F-16 Fighting Falcon

Pakistan
Pakistan Air Force

Poland
Polish Air Force
F-16 Fighting Falcon

Portugal
Portuguese Air Force
F-16 Fighting

Sweden
Swedish Air Force
Saab JAS 39 Gripen
Made under license as the Robot 99

Republic of China (Taiwan)
Republic of China Air Force
F-16 Fighting Falcon

Thailand
Royal Thai Air Force
Saab JAS 39 Gripen C/D
F-16 ADF Fighting Falcon

Turkey
Turkish Air Force
F-4 Phantom II
F-16 Fighting Falcon

United Arab Emirates
United Arab Emirates

39 Gripen

Israel
Israeli Air Force
F-15C Eagle
F-15I Strike Eagle (Ra'am)
F-16I Fighting Falcon (Sufa)

Italy
Italian Air Force
Eurofighter Typhoon
Italian Navy AV-8 Harrier II

Falcon

Saudi Arabia
Royal Saudi Air Force
F-15 Eagle
F-15S Strike Eagle

Singapore
Republic of Singapore Air Force
F-15SG Strike Eagle
F-16C/D Fighting Falcon
F-5S/T Tiger-II

Air Force F-16E/F Block 60

United Kingdom
Royal Air Force
Panavia Tornado ADV (retired)
Eurofighter Typhoon
Royal Navy Sea Harrier FA Mk.2 (retired)

United States
United States Air Force
F-15 Eagle
F-16 Fighting Falcon
F-22 Raptor
United States Navy F/A-18A+/C Hornet
F/A-18E/F Super Hornet
EA-18G Growler
U.S. Marine Corps F/A-18C/D Hornet
AV-8 Harrier II

Source http://en.wikipedia.org/wiki/AIM-120_AMRAAM

AIM-4 Falcon

AIM-4 Falcon

AIM-4 Falcon

A pair of AIM-4D Falcons in the weapons bay of the F-102 Delta Dagger fighter

Specifications

Length	1.98 m (6 ft 6 in)
Diameter	163 mm (6.4 in)
Warhead	3.4 kg (7.5 lb)
Wingspan	508 mm (20.0 in)
Propellant	solid fuel rocket
Operational range	9.7 km (6.0 mi)
Speed	Mach 3
Guidance system	semi-active radar homing and rear-aspect infrared homing

The **Hughes AIM-4 Falcon** was the first operational guided air-to-air missile of the United States Air Force. Development began in 1946; the weapon was first tested in 1949. The missile entered service with the USAF in 1956.

Produced in both heat-seeking and radar-guided versions, the missile served during the Vietnam War with USAF F-4 Phantom units. Designed to shoot down slow bombers with limited maneuverability, it was ineffective against maneuverable fighters over Vietnam. Lacking proximity fusing, the missile would only detonate if a direct hit was scored. Only five kills were recorded.

With the AIM-4's poor kill record rendering the F-4 ineffective at air-to-air combat, the fighters were modified to carry the AIM-9 Sidewinder missile instead. The Sidewinder was much more effective and continues to serve the armed forces of the United States to this day.

Development

Development of a guided air-to-air missile began in 1946. Hughes Aircraft was awarded a contract for a subsonic missile under the project designation **MX-798**, which soon gave way to the supersonic **MX-904** in 1947. The original purpose of the weapon was as a self-defense weapon for bomber aircraft, but after 1950 it was decided that it should arm fighter aircraft instead, particularly in the interception role.

The first test firings took place in 1949, at which time it was designated **AAM-A-2** and given the popular name **Falcon**. A brief policy of awarding fighter and bomber designations to missiles led it to be redesignated **F-98** in 1951. In 1955 the policy changed again, and the missile was again redesignated **GAR-1**.

The initial **GAR-1** and **GAR-2** models entered service in 1956. It armed the F-89 Scorpion, F-101B Voodoo and F-102 Delta Dagger interceptors. The only other users were Canada, Finland, Sweden and Switzerland, whose CF-101 Voodoo, Saab 35 Draken and Mirage II-IS carried the **AIM-4 Falcon**. Canada also hoped to use them on the CF-105 Arrow interceptor, that was never realized because of the Arrow's cancellation.

Fighters carrying the Falcon were often designed with internal weapons bays for carrying this missile. The Scorpion carried them on wingtip pods, while the Delta Dagger and Delta Dart had belly bays with a trapeze mechanism to move them into the airstream for launch (see picture above). The F-101B had an unusual bay arrangement where two were stored externally, and then the bay door would rotate to expose two more missiles. It is likely the F-111 internal bay would have accommodated the missile as well, but by the time of service, the Air Force had already dropped the Falcon for use against fighters, as well as the idea of using the F-111 as an air combat fighter.

The GAR-1 had semi-active radar homing (SARH), giving a range of about 5 miles (8 km). About 4,000 rounds were produced. It was replaced in production by the **GAR-1D** (later **AIM-4A**), with larger control surfaces. About 12,000 of this variant were produced, the major production version of the SARH Falcon.

The **GAR-2** (later **AIM-4B**) was a heat-seeker, generally limited to rear-aspect engagements, but with the advantage of being a 'fire and forget' weapon. As would also be Soviet practice, it was common to fire the weapon in salvos of both types to increase the chances of a hit (a heat-seeking missile fired first, followed moments later by a radar-guided missile). The GAR-2 was about 1.5 in (40 mm) longer and 16 lb (7 kg) heavier than its SARH counterpart. Its range was similar. It was replaced in production by the **GAR-2A** (later **AIM-4C**), with a more sensitive infrared seeker. A total of about 26,000 of the infrared-homing Falcons were built.

119th Fighter Wing weapons handlers with an AIM-4C, 1972.

AIM-9B and J next to HM-58 and AIM-4C
All used by the SwAF

All of the early Falcons had a small

7.6 lb (3.4 kg) warhead, limiting their lethal radius. Also limiting them tactically was the fact that Falcon lacked a proximity fuze: the fuzing for the missile was in the leading edges of the wings, requiring a direct hit to detonate.

In 1958 Hughes introduced a slightly enlarged version of the Falcon, initially dubbed **Super Falcon**, with a more powerful, longer-burning rocket engine, increasing speed and range. It had a larger warhead (28.7 lb / 13 kg) and better guidance systems. The SARH versions were **GAR-3** (**AIM-4E**) and the improved **GAR-3A** (**AIM-4F**). The infrared version was the **GAR-4A** (**AIM-4G**). About 2,700 SARH missiles and 3,400 IR Super Falcons were produced, replacing most earlier versions of the weapon in service.

The Falcon was redesignated **AIM-4** in September 1962.

The final version of the original Falcon was the **GAR-2B** (later **AIM-4D**), which entered service in 1963. This was intended as a fighter combat weapon, combining the lighter, smaller airframe of the earlier GAR-1/GAR-2 weapon with the improved IR seeker of the GAR-4A/AIM-4G.

A larger version of the Falcon carrying a 0.25-kiloton nuclear warhead was developed as the **GAR-11** (later designated the **AIM-26 Falcon**), while a long-range version was developed for the XF-108 Rapier and the Lockheed YF-12 interceptors as the **GAR-9** (later **AIM-47 Falcon**).

Operational history

The Air Force deployed AIM-4 in May 1967 during the Vietnam War on the new F-4D Phantom II, which carried it on the inner wing pylons and was not wired to carry the AIM-9 Sidewinder. The missile's combat performance was very poor. The Falcon, already operational on Air Defense Command aircraft, was designed to be used against bombers and its slow seeker cooling times requiring as much as 6 to 7 seconds to obtain a lock on a target rendered it largely ineffective against maneuvering fighters. Moreover it could only be cooled once. Limited coolant supply meant that once cooled, the missile would expend its supply of liquid nitrogen in two minutes, rendering it useless on the rail. The missile also had a small warhead, and lacked proximity fusing. As a result, only five kills were scored, all with the AIM-4D version. (The Falcon was also experimentally fired by the F-102 Delta Dagger against ground targets at night using its infrared seeker.)

A New Jersey ANG F-106A launching an AIM-4, 1984.

The weapon was unpopular with pilots from the onset and was formally withdrawn in 1969, to be replaced in the F-4D by the Sidewinder after retrofitting the proper wiring. Col. Robin Olds, commanding the F-4 Phantom II-equipped 8th Tactical Fighter Wing, was an outspoken critic of the missile and said of it:

By the beginning of June, we all hated the new AIM-4 Falcon missiles. I loathed the damned useless things. I wanted my Sidewinders back. In two missions I had fired seven or eight of the bloody things and not one guided. They were worse than I had anticipated. Sometimes they refused to launch; sometimes they just cruised off into the blue without guiding. In the thick of an engagement with my head twisting and turning, trying to keep track of friend and foe, I'd forget which of the four I had (already) selected and couldn't tell which of the remaining was perking and which head was already expiring on its launch rail. Twice upon returning to base I had the tech rep go over the switchology and firing sequences. We never discovered I was doing anything wrong.

Col. Olds became exasperated with the Falcon's poor combat performance. He ordered his entire fighter wing rewire the F-4D's to carry more reliable Sidewinders. Although it was an unauthorized field modification, the entire air force eventually followed his example. An effort to address the limitations of AIM-4D led to the development in 1970 of the **XAIM-4H**, which had a laser proximity fuze, new warhead, and better maneuverability. It was cancelled the following year without entering service.

The AIM-4F/AIM-4G Super Falcon remained in USAF and ANG service, primarily with F-102 Delta Dagger and F-106 Delta Dart interceptors, until the final retirement of the F-106 in 1988.

The AIM-4C was also produced as the **HM-58** for the Swiss Air Force for use on Dassault Mirage IIIS, and license-manufactured in Sweden for the Swedish Air Force (as the **Rb 28**) to equip the Saab 35 Draken and the Saab 37 Viggen. The seeker of the missile was also re-designed.

Operators

🇨🇦 **Canada**
Royal Canadian Air Force
Canadian Forces

🇫🇮 **Finland**
Finnish Air Force - (Swedish built missiles)

🇸🇪 **Sweden**
Swedish Air Force - (Licence built by SAAB)

🇨🇭 **Switzerland**
Swiss Air Force

🇺🇸 **United States**
United States Air Force

🇬🇷 **Greece**
Hellenic Air Force

🇹🇷 **Turkey**
Turkish Air Force

Specifications (GAR-1D/ -2B / AIM-4C/D)

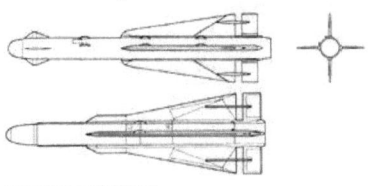

Hughes AIM-4A and AIM-4G Falcon

Length: 78 in (2.0 m) / 79.5 in (2.02 m)
Wingspan: 20 in (510 mm)
Diameter: 6.4 in (160 mm)
Weight: 119 lb (54 kg) / 135 lb (61 kg)
Speed: Mach 3
Range 6 mi (9.7 km)
Guidance: semi-active radar homing / rear-aspect infrared
Warhead: 7.6 lb (3.4 kg) high explosive
Source http://en.wikipedia.org/wiki/AIM-4_Falcon

AIM-9 Sidewinder

AIM-9 Sidewinder

An AIM-9 Sidewinder is affixed to a U.S. Navy F/A-18 Hornet on board the USS *George Washington* (CVN-73), in February 1998.

Type	Short-range air-to-air missile
Place of origin	United States
Service history	
In service	1956 (AIM-9B) – presen
Production history	
Manufacturer	Nammo
	Raytheon Company
	Ford Aerospace
	Loral Corp.
Unit cost	US$85,000
Produced	September 1953
Specifications	
Weight	188 pounds (85.3 kg)
Length	9 feet 11 inches (3.02 m)
Diameter	5 in (127.0 mm)
Warhead	WDU-17/B annular blast frag
Warhead weight	20.8 lb (9.4 kg)
Detonation mechanism	Magnetic influence (old models)
	Active infrared (AIM-9L onwards)
Engine	Hercules/Bermite MK 36 Solid-fuel rocket
Wingspan	11 in (279.4 mm)
Operational range	0.6 to 22 miles (1.0 to 35.4 km)
Speed	Mach 2.5
Guidance system	Infrared homing
Launch platform	Aircraft, helicopter gunships

The **AIM-9 Sidewinder** is an infrared homing, short-range, air-to-air missile carried mostly by fighter aircraft and recently, certain gunship helicopters. The missile entered service with the United States Navy in the mid-1950s, and variants and upgrades remain in active service with many air forces after five decades. The United States Air Force purchased the Sidewinder after the missile was developed by the United States Navy at China Lake, California.

The Sidewinder is the most widely used missile in the West, with more than 110,000 missiles produced for the U.S. and 27 other nations, of which perhaps one percent have been used in combat. It has been built under license by some other nations including Sweden. The AIM-9 is one of the oldest, least expensive, and most successful air-to-air missiles, with an estimated 270 aircraft kills in its history of use.

The missile was designed to be simple to upgrade. It has been said that the design goals for the original Sidewinder were to produce a reliable and effective missile with the "electronic complexity of a table model radio and the mechanical complexity of a washing machine"—goals which were well accomplished in the early missiles. The United States Navy hosted a 50th anniversary celebration of its existence in 2002. Boeing won a contract in March 2010 to support Sidewinder operations through 2055, guaranteeing that the weapons system will remain in operation until at least that date. Air Force Spokeswoman Stephanie Powell noted that due to its relative low cost, versatility, and reliability it is "very possible that the Sidewinder will remain in Air Force inventories through the late 21st century."

Launch sequence

When a Sidewinder missile is being launched, most pilots including NATO pilots use the brevity code **Fox Two** in radio communication, as with all "heat-seeking" missiles.

Name selection

Sidewinder is the common name of *Crotalus cerastes*, a venomous rattlesnake which uses infrared sensory organs to hunt warm-blooded prey. Early versions of the missile tended to perform zig-zagging course corrections during the early part of their flight path, following a trajectory that resembled the sidewinding motion of the snake.

History

The development of the Sidewinder missile began in 1946 at the Naval Ordnance Test Station (NOTS), Inyokern, California, now the Naval Air Weapons Station China Lake, California as an in-house research project conceived by William B. McLean. McLean initially called his effort "Local Fuze Project 602" using laboratory funding, volunteer help and fuze funding to develop what it called a heat-homing rocket. It did not receive official funding until 1951 when the effort was mature enough to show to Admiral William "Deak" Parsons, the Deputy Chief of the Bureau of Ordnance (BuOrd). It subsequently received designation as a program in 1952. The Sidewinder introduced several new technologies that made it simpler and much more reliable than its United States Air Force (USAF) counterpart, the AIM-4 Falcon, under development during the same period. After disappointing experiences with the Falcon in the Vietnam War, the Air Force replaced its Falcons with Sidewinders.

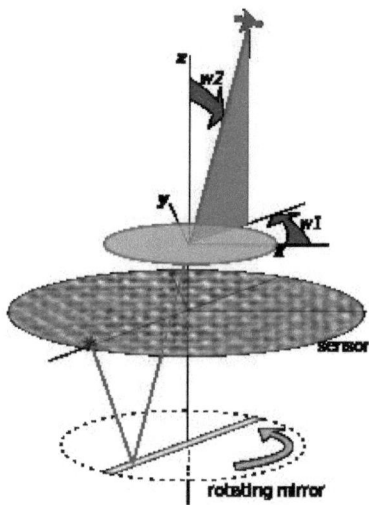

Geometric arrangement of mirror, IR detector and target.[citation needed]

The Sidewinder incorporated a number of innovations over the independently developed World War II German Missile Enzian's "Madrid" IR range fuze that enabled it to be successful. The first innovation was to replace the "steering" mirror with a forward-facing mirror rotating around a shaft pointed out the front of the missile. The detector was mounted in front of the mirror. When the long axis of the mirror, the missile axis and the line of sight to the target all fell in the same plane, the reflected rays from the target reached the detector (provided the target was not very far off axis). Therefore, the angle of the mirror at the instant of detection ($w1$) estimated the direction of the target in the roll axis of the missile.

An AIM-9B hitting an F6F-5K drone at China Lake, 1957.

The yaw/pitch (angle $w2$) direction of the target depended on how far to the outer edge of the mirror the target was. [citation needed] If the target was further off axis, the rays reaching the detector would be reflected from the outer edge of the mirror. If the target was closer on axis, the rays would be reflected from closer to the centre of the mirror. Rotating on a fixed shaft, the mirror's linear speed was higher at the outer edge. Therefore if a target was further off-axis its "flash" in the detector occurred for a briefer time, or longer if it was closer to the center. The off-axis angle could then be estimated by the duration of the reflected pulse of infrared.

The Sidewinder also included a dramatically improved guidance algorithm. The Enzian attempted to fly directly at its target, feeding the direction of the telescope into the control system as it if were a joystick. This meant the missile always flew directly at its target, and under most conditions would end up behind it, "chasing" it down. This meant that the missile had to have enough of a speed advantage over its target that it did not run out of fuel during the interception.

The Sidewinder is not guided on the actual position recorded by the detector, but on the *change* in position since the last sighting. So if the target remained at 5 degrees left between two rotations of the mirror, the electronics would not output any signal to the control system. Consider a missile fired at right angles to its target; if the missile is flying at the same speed as the target it should "lead" it by 45 degrees, flying to an impact point far in front of where the target was when it was fired. If the missile is traveling four times the speed of the target, it should follow an angle about 11 degrees in front. In either case, the missile should keep that angle all the way to interception, which means that the angle that the target makes against the detector is constant. It was this constant angle that the Sidewinder attempted to maintain. This "proportional pursuit" system is very easy to implement, yet it offers high-performance lead calculation almost for free and can respond to changes in the target's flight path, which is much more efficient and makes the missile "lead" the target.

However this system also requires the missile to have a fixed roll axis orientation. If the missile spins at all, the timing based on the speed of rotation of the mirror is no longer accurate. Correcting for this spin would normally require some sort of sensor to tell which way is "down" and then adding controls to correct it. Instead, small control surfaces were placed at the rear of the missile with spinning disks on their outer surface; these are known as rollerons. Airflow over the disk spins them to a high speed. If the missile starts to roll, the gyroscopic force of the disk drives the control surface into the airflow, cancelling the motion. Thus the Sidewinder team replaced a potentially complex control system with a simple mechanical solution.

Test pilot Wally Schirra

Wally Schirra was an early Sidewinder test pilot when he was stationed at NOTS between 1952 to 1954. During one flight, Schirra fired the Sidewinder missile and the missile "doubled back" and started to chase his jet. Schirra, through skillful flying, avoided the Sidewinder. He later went onto to join NASA Mercury program as one of the first seven astronauts to fly into space.

Flight test and service introduction

Prototype Sidewinder-1 missile on an AD-4 Skyraider during flight testing

A prototype Sidewinder, the **XAAM-N-7** (later **AIM-9A**), was first fired successfully in September 1953. The initial production version, designated **AAM-N-7** (later **AIM-9B**), entered operational use in 1956, and has been improved upon steadily since.

Combat debut

The first combat use of the Sidewinder was on September 24, 1958, with the air force of the Republic of China (Taiwan), during the Second Taiwan Strait Crisis. During that period of time, ROC F-86 Sabres were routinely engaged in air battles with the People's Republic of China over the Taiwan Strait. The PRC MiG-17s had higher altitude ceiling performance and in similar fashion to Korean War encounters between the F-86 and earlier MiG-15, the PRC formations cruised above the ROC Sabres, immune to their .50 cal weaponry and only choosing battle when conditions favored them. In a highly secret effort, United States provided a few dozen Sidewinders to ROC forces and an Aviation Ordnance Team from the U. S. Marine Corps, led by Marine Captain P. L. Lockaby (at the time one of the very few persons in the world with expertise regarding the then brand-new missile), to modify their Sabres to carry the Sidewinder. In the first encounter on 24 September 1958, the Sidewinders were used to ambush the MiG-17s as they flew past the Sabres thinking they were invulnerable to attack. The MiGs broke formation and descended to the altitude of the Sabres in swirling dogfights. This action marked the first successful use of air-to-air missiles in combat in history, and the downed MiG's as their first casualties. Captain Lockaby was awarded the Navy Commendation Medal.

Compromised technology

The Taiwan Strait battles inadvertently produced a new derivative of Sidewinder. Shortly after that conflict the Soviet Union began the manufacture of the K-13/R-3S missile (NATO reporting name **AA-2 'Atoll'**), a reverse-engineered copy of the Sidewinder. It was made possible after a Taiwanese AIM-9B hit a Chinese Communist MiG-17 without exploding, the missile lodging itself in the airframe of the MiG after which the pilot was able to bring both plane and missile back to base. According to Ron Westrum in his book "Sidewinder", the Soviets obtained the plans for Sidewinder from a Swedish Air Force Colonel, Stig Wennerström, and rushed their version into service by 1961 copying it so closely that even the part numbers were duplicated, although none of the known Soviet sources mention this. Years later, Soviet engineers would admit that the captured Sidewinder served as a "university course" in missile design and substantially improved Soviet and allied air-to-air capabilities. In 1972, when the Finnish Air Force started using Sidewinder (AIM-9P) in their Saab 35 Draken fighters, they were already using Soviet-made Atoll in their MiG-21s; Finns found the two so similar that they tested Sidewinders in MiGs and Atolls in Drakens.

USAF adoption

Although originally developed for the USN and a competitor to the USAF AIM-4 Falcon, the Sidewinder was subsequently introduced into USAF service when DoD directed that the F-4 Phantom be adopted by the USAF. The Air Force originally borrowed F-4B model Phantoms, which were equipped with AIM-9B Sidewinders as the short-range armament. The first production USAF Phantoms were the F-4C model, which carried the AIM-9B Sidewinder. The Air Force opted to carry only AIM-4 Falcon on their F-4D model Phantoms introduced to Vietnam service in 1967, but disappointment with combat use of the Falcon led to a crash effort to reconfigure the F-4D so that it could carry Sidewinders. The USAF nomenclature for the Sidewinder was the **GAR-8** (later **AIM-9E**). During the 1960s the USN and USAF pursued their own separate versions of the Sidewinder, but cost considerations later forced the development of common variants beginning with the AIM-9L.

Continued evolution

(Top: AIM-9A; Bottom: AIM-9C) Early Sidewinders mounted on an F-8D Crusader.

(From top to bottom) The U.S. Navy's AIM-9B, AIM-9D, and AIM-9C in the early 1970s

The Sidewinder subsequently evolved through a series of upgraded versions with newer, more sensitive seekers with various types of cooling and various propulsion, fuse, and warhead improvements. Although each of those versions had various seeker, cooling, and fusing differences, all but one shared infrared homing. The exception was the U.S. Navy **AAM-N-7 Sidewinder IB** (later **AIM-9C**), a Sidewinder with a semi-active radar homing seeker head developed for the F-8 Crusader. Only about 1,000 of these weapons were produced, many of which were later rebuilt as the AGM-122 Sidearm anti-radiation missile.

Vietnam influence on Sidewinder development

When air combat started over North Vietnam in 1965, Sidewinder was the standard short range missile carried by the US Navy on its F-4 Phantom and F-8 Crusader fighters and could be carried on the A-4 Skyhawk and on the A-7 Corsair for self-defense. The Air Force also used the Sidewinder on its F-4C Phantoms and when MiGs began challenging strike groups, the F-105 Thunderchief also carried the Sidewinder for self-defense. Performance of the Sidewinder and the AIM-7 Sparrow was not as satisfactory as hoped and both the Navy and Air Force studied their performance of their aircrews, aircraft, weapons and training as well as supporting infrastructure. The Air Force conducted the classified Red Baron Report while the Navy conducted a study concentrating primarily on performance of air-to-air weapons that was unofficially called and better known as the "Ault Report". The impact of both was modifications to the Sidewinder by both services to improve its ability to perform in the demanding air-to-air arena and increase reliability.

Summary of Vietnam War AIM-9 aerial combat kills 1965-1973

USN AIM-9 Sidewinder aerial combat kills:

Missile firing aircraft	AIM-9 Sidewinder model (Type)	Aircraft downed	Comme
F-8E Crusader	AIM-9D	(1) MiG-21/(9) MiG-17s	US Fighters launched from US aircraft carriers; Hancock 19, USS Oriskany 34, USS Bon Homme Richard 31, USS Ticonde CV 14
F-8C	AIM-9D	(3) MiG-17s/(1) MiG-21	US Fighters launched from USS Bon Homme Richard
F-8H	AIM-9D	(2) MiG-21s	US Fighters launched from USS Bon Homme Richard
F-4B Phantom II	AIM-9D	(2) MiG-17s/(2) MiG-21s	US Fighters launched from USS Constellation CV-64 and USS Kitty Hawk
F-4J	AIM-9D	(2) MiG-21s	US Fighters launched from USS America 66 and Constell
F-4B	AIM-9B	(1) MiG-17	US Fighters launched from USS Kitty Hawk
F-4B	AIM-9G	(7) MiG-17s/(2) MiG-19s	Fighters launched from USS Coral Sea CV-43 and USS Mi CV-41
F-4J	AIM-9G	(7) MiG-17s/(7) MiG-21s	Fighters launched from USS Enterprise CVN-65 USS America USS San CV-60, Constell USS Kitty Hawk
Total MiG-17s	29	Total MiG-21s	15

USAF AIM-9 Sidewinder aerial combat kills:

Missile firing aircraft	Sidewinder AIM-9 Model (Type)	Aircraft downed	Con
F-4C	AIM-9B	(13) MiG-17s/(9) MiG-21s	45th Tact Figh Squ (TFS 389t TFS 390t TFS 433t TFS 480t TFS 555t
F-105D Thunderchief	AIM-9B	(3) MiG-17s	333t TFS 469t
F-4D	AIM-9E	(2) MiG-21s	13th 469t
F-4E	AIM-9E	(4) MiG-21s	13th 34th 35th 469t
F-4D	AIM-9J	(2) MiG-19s/(1) MiG-21	523t TFS 555t
Total MiG-17s	16	Total MiG-21s	16

Navy AIM-9D/G/H

AIM-9Ds armed F-4B of VF-111 on the USS *Coral Sea*.

The Navy Sidewinder design progression went from the early production B model to the D model that was used extensively in Vietnam. The G and H models followed with new forward canard design improving ACM performance and expanded acquisition modes and improved envelopes. The "Hotel" model followed shortly after the "Golf" and featured a solid state design that improved reliability in the carrier environment where shock from catapult launches and arrested landings had a deteriorating effect on the earlier vacuum tube designs. The Ault report had a strong impact on Sidewinder design, manufacture, and handling.

Air Force AIM-9E/J/N/P
Once the Air Force adopted the Sidewinder as part of its arsenal, it developed the AIM-9E, introducing it in 1967. The "Echo" was an improved version of the basic AIM-9B featuring larger forward canards as well as a more aerodynamic IR seeker and an improved rocket motor. The missile, however still had to be fired at the rear quarter of the target, a drawback of all early IR missiles. Significant upgrades were applied to the first true dogfight version, the AIM-9J, which was rushed to the South-East Asia Theatre in July 1972 during the Linebacker campaign, in which many aerial encounters with North Vietnamese MiGs occurred. The Juliet model could be launched at up to 7.5g (74 m/s^2) and introduced the first solid state components and improved actuators capable of delivering 90 lb·ft (120 N·m) torque to the canards, thereby improving dogfight prowess. In 1973, Ford began production of an enhanced AIM-9J-1, which was later redesignated the AIM-9N. The AIM-9J was widely exported. The J/N evolved into the P series, with five versions being produced (P1 to P5) including such improvements as new fuzes, reduced-smoke rocket motors, and all-aspect capability on the latest P4 and P5. BGT in Germany has developed a conversion kit for upgrading AIM-9J/N/P guidance and control assemblies to the AIM-9L standard, and this is being marketed as AIM-9JULI. The core of this upgrade is the fitting of the DSQ-29 seeker unit of the AIM-9L, replacing the original J/N/P seeker to give improved capabilities.

All-aspect Sidewinders

AIM-9L
The next major advance in IR Sidewinder development was the **AIM-**

AIM-9L Captive air training missile with part/section in blue color, denoting inert warhead and rocket motor, for training purposes.

9L ("Lima") model, introduced in 1978. This was the first "all-aspect" Sidewinder with the ability to attack from all directions, including head-on, which had a dramatic effect on close in combat tactics. Its first combat use was by a pair of US Navy F-14s in the Gulf of Sidra in 1981 versus two Libyan Su-22 Fitters, both of the latter being destroyed by AIM-9Ls. Its first use in actual warfare was by the United Kingdom during the 1982 Falklands War, the "Lima" reportedly achieved a kill ratio of around 80%, a dramatic improvement over the 10-15% levels of earlier versions scoring 17 and 2 shared kills against Argentine aircraft. On that same year but over Lebanon's Bekaa Valley, 51 out of the 55 Syrian-flown MiGs shot down were hit by Israeli Air Force Sidewinders.

In both combat uses of AIM-9L, the opponents had not developed any tactics for the evasion of a head-on missile shot of this kind, making them more vulnerable. The AIM-9L was also the first Sidewinder that was a joint variant used by both the US Navy and Air Force since the AIM-9B. The "Lima" was distinguished from earlier Sidewinder variants by its double delta forward canard configuration and natural metal finish of the guidance and control section. The Lima was also built under license in Europe by a team headed by Diehl BGT Defence. There are a number of "Lima" variants in operational service at present. First developed was the 9L Tactical, which is an upgraded version of the basic 9L missile.

Next was the 9L Genetic, which has increased infra-red counter counter measures (IRCCM); this upgrade consisted of a removable module in the Guidance Control Section (GCS) which provided flare-rejection capability. Next came the 9L(I), which had its IRCCM module hardwired into the GCS, providing improved countermeasures as well as an upgraded seeker system. Diehl BGT also markets the AIM-9L(I)-1 which again upgrades the 9L(I)GCS and is considered an operational equivalent to the initially "US only" AIM-9M.

AIM-9M

AIM-9M Sidewinder with distinctive "Dash-9" lettering being preflighted by a USAF pilot. Note the blue stripe, which indicates that this example has an inert warhead intended for training purposes

The subsequent **AIM-9M ("Mike")** has the all-aspect capability of the L model while providing all-around higher performance. The M model has improved capability against infrared countermeasures, enhanced background discrimination capability, and a reduced-smoke rocket motor. These modifications increase its ability to locate and lock-on to a target and decrease the chance of missile detection. Deliveries of the initial AIM-9M-1 began in 1982. The only changes from the AIM-9L to the AIM-9M were related to the Guidance Control Section (GCS). Several models were introduced in pairs with even numbers designating Navy versions and odd for USAF: AIM-9M-2/3, AIM-9M-4/5, and AIM-9M-6/7 which was rushed to the Persian Gulf area during Desert Shield to address specific threats expected to be present. The AIM-9M-8/9 incorporated replacement of five circuit cards and the related parentboard to update infrared counter counter measures (IRCCM) capability to improve 9M capability against the latest threat IRCM. The first AIM-9M-8/9 modifications, fielded in 1995, involved deskinning the guidance section and substitution of circuit cards at the depot level, which is labor-intensive and expensive—as well as removing missiles from inventory during the upgrade period. The AIM-9X concept is to use reprogrammable software to permit upgrades without disassembly.

Further development

AIM-9R

AIM-9R test firing from an F/A-18C at Naval Air Weapons Station China Lake

The Navy began development of AIM-9R, a Sidewinder seeker upgrade in 1987 that featured a Focal Plane Array (FPA) seeker using video-camera type charge-coupled device (CCD) detectors and featuring increased off-boresight capability. The technology at the time was restricted to visual (daylight) use only and the USAF did not agree on this requirement, preferring another technology path. AIM-9R reached flight test stage before it was cancelled and subsequently both services agreed to join a joint development of the AIM-9X variant.

BOA/Boxoffice

China Lake developed an improved compressed carriage control configuration titled BOA. ("Compressed carriage" missiles have smaller control surfaces to allow more missiles to fit in a given space. The surfaces may be permanently "clipped", or may fold out when the missile is launched.)

The BOA design reduced size of con-

Testing compressed carriage Sidewinder BOA configuration at China Lake

trol surfaces, eliminating the rollerons, and returned to simple forward-canard design. Although the Navy and Air Force had jointly developed and procured AIM-9L/M, BOA was a Navy-only effort supported by internal China Lake Independent Research & Development (IR&D) funding. Meanwhile, the Air Force was pursuing a parallel effort to develop a compressed carriage version of Sidewinder, called Boxoffice, for the F-22. The Joint Chiefs of Staff directed that the services collaborate on AIM-9X, which ended these separate efforts. The results of BOA and Boxoffice were provided to the industry teams competing for AIM-9X, and elements of both can be found in the AIM-9X design.

AIM-9X

After looking at advanced short range missile designs during the AIM portion of the ACEVAL/AIMVAL Joint Test and Evaluation at Nellis AFB in the 1974-78 timeframe, the Air Force and Navy agreed on the need for the Advanced Medium Range Air-to-Air Missile AMRAAM. But agreement over development of an Advanced Short Range Air-to-Air Missile ASRAAM was problematic and disagreement between the Air Force and Navy over design concepts (Air Force had developed AIM-82 and Navy had flight-tested Agile and flown it in AIMVAL). Congress eventually insisted the services work on a joint effort resulting in the AIM-9M, thereby compromising without exploring the improved off boresight and kinematic capability potential offered by Agile. In 1985, the Soviet Union did field a solid rocket motor (SRM) missile (AA-11 Archer/R-73) that was very similar to Agile. At that point, the Soviet Union took the lead in SRM technology and correspondingly fielded improved InfraRed Counter Measures (IRCM) to defeat or reduce the effectiveness of the latest Sidewinders. With the reunification of Germany and improved relations in the aftermath of the Soviet Union, the West became aware of how potent both the AA-11 and IRCM were and SRM requirements were readdressed.

The first guided launch of an AIM-9X occurred in 1999 from a VX-9 F/A-18C and shot-down a QF-4 Drone

For a brief period in the late 1980s, an ASRAAM effort led by a European consortium was in play under a MOA with the United States in which AMRAAM development would be led by the US and ASRAAM by the Europeans. The UK working with the aft end of the ASRAAM and Germany developing the seeker (Germany had firsthand experience improving the Sidewinder seeker of the AIM-9J/AIM-9F). By 1990, technical and funding issues had stymied ASRAAM and the problem appeared stalled, so in light of the threat of AA-11 and improved IRCM, the US embarked on determining requirements for AIM-9X as a counter to both the AA-11 and improved IRCM features. The first draft of the requirement was ready by 1991 and the primary competitors were Raytheon and Hughes. Later, the UK resolved to revive the ASRAAM development and selected Hughes to provide the seeker technology in the form of a high off-boresight capable Focal Plane Array. However, the UK did not choose to improve the turning kinematic capability of ASRAAM to compete with AA-11. As part of the AIM-9X program, the US conducted a foreign cooperative test of the ASRAAM seeker to evaluate its potential, and an advanced version featuring improved kinematics was proposed as part of the AIM-9X competition. In the end, the Hughes-evolved Sidewinder design, featuring virtually the same British funded seeker as used by ASRAAM, was selected as the winner.

An AIM-9X on an 422d Test & Evaluation Squadron F-15C, 2002.

The **AIM-9X** Sidewinder, developed by Raytheon engineers, entered service in November 2003 with the USAF (lead platform is the F-15C; the USN lead platform is the F/A-18C) and is a substantial upgrade to the Sidewinder family featuring an imaging infrared focal plane array (FPA) seeker with claimed 90° off-boresight capability, compatibility with helmet-mounted displays such as the new U.S. Joint Helmet Mounted Cueing System, and a totally new three-dimensional thrust-vectoring control (TVC) system providing increased turn capability over traditional control surfaces. Utilizing the JHMCS, a pilot can point the AIM-9X missile's seeker and "lock on" by simply looking at a target, thereby increasing air combat effectiveness. It retains the same rocket motor, fuze and warhead of the 9-"Mike", but its lower drag gives it improved range and speed. AIM-9X also includes an internal cooling system, eliminating the need for use of launch-rail nitrogen bottles (U.S. Navy and Marines) or internal argon bottle (USAF). It also features an electronic safe and arm device similar to the AMRAAM, allowing reduction in minimum range and reprogrammable InfraRed Counter Counter Measures (IR-CCM) capability that coupled with the FPA provide improved look down into clutter and performance against the latest IRCM. Though not part of the original requirement, AIM-9X demonstrated potential for a Lock-on After Launch capability, allowing for possible internal use for the F-35, F-22 Raptor and even in a submarine-launched configuration for use against ASW platforms. The AIM-9X has been tested for a surface attack capability, with mixed results.

As of September 2008, Raytheon has delivered 3,000 AIM-9X missiles to the armed services and has begun testing the Block II version of the missile. The Block II adds Lock-on After Launch capability with a datalink, so the missile can be launched first and then directed to its target afterwards by an aircraft with the proper equipment for 360 degree engagements, such as the F-35 and F-22. By January 2013, the AIM-9X Block II was about halfway through its operational testing and performing better than expected. NAVAIR reported that the missile was exceeding performance requirements in all areas, including lock-on after launch (LOAL). The Block II performed as designed in 21 of 22 combined developmental and live fire tests, with 17 of the tests resulting in the missile guiding to a lethal target intercept in aggressive scenarios. Since the beginning of operational testing, 5 of 7 live fire attempts had guided to a lethal target intercept. One area where the Block II needs improvement is helmetless high off-boresight (HHOBS) performance. It is functioning well on the missile, but performance is less superior than in the Block I AIM-9X. The HHOBS deficiency does not impact any other Block II capabilities, and is planning to be improved upon by a software clean-up build. Objectives of the operational test are due to be completed by the third quarter of 2013.

Extended Range

In September 2012, Raytheon was ordered to continue developing the Sidewinder into a possible Block III variant. The new missile will have a longer range (unspecified), modern components to replace old ones, and an insensitive munitions warhead, which is more stable and less likely to detonate by accident, making it safer for ground crews.

Design

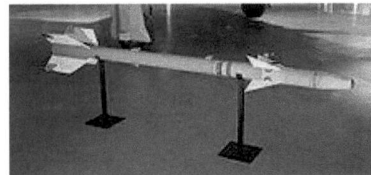

An AIM-9E Sidewinder missile on display at the National Air and Space Museum

The AIM-9 is made up of a number of different components manufactured by different companies, including Aerojet and Raytheon. The missile is divided into four main sections: guidance, target detector, warhead, and rocket motor.

The Guidance and Control Unit (GCU) contains most of the electronics and mechanics that enable the missile to function. At the very front is the IR seeker head utilizing the rotating reticle, mirror, and five CdS cells or "pan and scan" focal-plane array (AIM-9X), electric motor, and armature, all protruding into a glass dome. Directly behind this are the electronics that gather data, interpret signals, and generate the control signals that steer the missile. An umbilical on the side of the GCU attaches to the launcher, which detaches from the missile at launch. To cool the seeker head, a 5,000 psi (35 MPa) argon bottle (TMU-72/B or A/B) is carried internally in Air Force AIM-9L/M variants while the Navy uses a rail mounted nitrogen bottle. The AIM-9X model contains a Stirling cryo-engine to cool the seeker elements. Two electric servos power the canards to steer the missile (except AIM-9X). At the back of the GCU is a gas grain generator or thermal battery (AIM-9X) to provide electrical power. The AIM-9X features High-Off-Boresight capability; together with JHMCS (Joint Helmet Mounted Cueing System), this missile is capable of locking on to a target that is in its field of regard said to be up to 90 degrees off boresight. The AIM-9X has several unique design features including built-in-test to aid in maintenance and reliability, an electronic safe and arm device, an additional digital umbilical similar to the AMRAAM and jet vane control.

Next is a target detector with four IR emitters and detectors that detect if the target is moving farther away. When it detects this action taking place, it sends a signal to the Warhead Safe and Arm device to detonate the warhead. Versions older than the AIM-9L featured an influence fuze that relied on the target's magnetic field as input. Current trends in shielded wires and non-magnetic metals in aircraft construction rendered this obsolete.

A Sidewinder hitting a QF-4B drone, 1974.

The AIM-9H model contained a 25-pound (11 kg) expanding rod-blast fragmentary warhead. All other models up to the AIM-9M contained a 22-pound (10 kg) annular blast fragmentary warhead. The missile's warhead rods can break rotor blades (an immediately fatal event for any helicopter).

Recent models of the AIM-9 are configured with an annular blast fragmentation warhead, the WDU-17B by Argotech Corporation. The case is made of spirally wound spring steel filled with 8 pounds (4 kg) of PBXN-3 explosive. The warhead features a safe/arm device requiring five seconds at 20 g (~200 m/s²) acceleration before the fuze is armed, giving a minimum range of approximately 2.5 kilometers.

The Mk36 solid propellant rocket motor provides propulsion for the missile. A reduced smoke propellant makes it difficult for a target to see and avoid the missile. This section also features the launch lugs used to hold the missile to the rail of the missile launcher. The forward of the three lugs has two contact buttons that electrically activate the motor igniter. The fins provide stability from an aerodynamic point of view, but it is the "rollerons" at the end of the wings providing gyroscopic precession that prevents the serpentine motion that gave the Sidewinder its name in the early days. The wings and fins of the AIM-9X are much smaller to accommodate one in each side bay of the F-22 Raptor as originally planned, AIM-9X control surfaces are reversed from earlier Sidewinders with the control section located in the rear, while the wings up front provide stability. The AIM-9X also features vectored thrust or jet vane control to increase maneuverability and accuracy, with four vanes inside the exhaust that move as the fins move. The last upgrade to the missile motor on the AIM-9X is the addition of a wire harness that allows communication between the guidance section and the control section, as well as a new 1760 bus to connect the guidance section with the launcher's digital umbilical.

Other Sidewinder developments

TC-1 Republic of China (Taiwan)

The TC-1 is a Taiwanese development of the AIM-9L originally meant to arm the ROCAF's indigenous F-CK-1 fighter. A ground-launched version was since developed as part of the Antelope Air Defense System, being carried on a Humvee-based launcher vehicle. The Pelican-Hardigg Technical Packaging division of Pelican Products Inc. has designed, qualified, and now manufactures a single missile AUR (All Up Round) Container for this missile. The Pelican-Hardigg Missile Container has been designed to be light enough for the loaded container to be physically handled by 6 men.

Chaparral

A version for the U.S. Army with a launcher for four AIM-9D missiles mounted on a tracked vehicle and called the MIM-72/M48 Chaparral was also developed. In this configuration an operator sat in a protected capsule that was incorporated into the launcher assembly that rotated as an integrated unit. The Chaparral was introduced into service in 1969 and remained an integral part of the Army's air defense network until 1998.

AGM-122A Sidearm

The Sidewinder was also the basis for the **AGM-122A Sidearm** anti-radiation missile utilizing an AIM-9C guidance section modified to detect and track a radiating ground-based air defense system radar. The target-detecting device is modified for air-to-surface use, employing forward hemisphere acquisition capability. Sidearm stocks have apparently been expended, and the weapon is no longer in the active inventory.

Experimental use of an AIM-9L against tanks at China Lake, 1971.

Anti-tank variant

China Lake experimented with Sidewinder in the air-to-ground mode including use as an anti-tank weapon. Starting from 2008, the AIM-9X demonstrated its ability as a successful light air-to-ground missile.

Larger rocket motor

Under the High Altitude Project, engineers at China Lake mated a Sidewinder warhead and seeker to a Sparrow rocket motor to experiment with usefulness of a larger motor.

Operators

Argentina - AIM-9Bs in the navy A-4C/Q Skyhawks (retired) and AIM-9L/M in air force A-4AR

Australia - AIM-9X used by F/A-18F Super Hornets

- Austria - *replaced by IRIS-T*
- Belgium - *AIM-9M for F-16AM/BM Fighting Falcon*
- Bahrain - *AIM-9P for F-5E Tiger II, AIM-9L for F-16C*
- Brazil - *AIM-9B replaced by MAA-1 Piranha of the Brazilian Air Force, however the Brazilian Naval Aviation still uses the AIM-9H*
- Cameroon - *used AIM-9B.*
- Canada
- Chile - *received AIM-9Bs and Js for the F-5E Tiger II in 1976, has used AIM-9Ps since the 1980s, in 2007 received for F-16 Block 50/52 plus AIM-9Ms*
- Colombia
- Czech Republic
- Denmark
- Egypt
- Ethiopia
- Finland
- France - *AIM-9Bs - replaced by R550 Magic*
- Germany - *replaced by IRIS-T*
- Greece - *replaced by IRIS-T*
- Hungary - used on JAS-39 Gripen
- Indonesia, used on Northrop F-5, F-16 Fighting Falcon and Bae Hawk
- Iran
- Iraq - *Iraq Ordered 200 AIM-9L/M-8/9 with their new F-16IQs*
- Israel
- Italy - *replaced by IRIS-T*
- Japan - used on Boeing F-15 Eagle, Mitsubishi F-1, Mitsubishi F-2, McDonnell Douglas F-4 Phantom II, Lockheed F-104 Starfighter (retired), North American F-86 Sabre (retired).
- Jordan
- Kuwait
- Malaysia
- Mexico - used on F-5
- Morocco
- Netherlands - AIM-9M and AIM-9X on F-16 Fighting Falcon
- New Zealand - used on RNZAF A-4 Skyhawk, no longer in use
- Norway - *replaced by IRIS-T*
- Oman
- Pakistan - *AIM-9B: F-86, F-6. AIM-9P/L: F-16A/B, F-6, F-7P/PG, Mirage III/V, JF-17. AIM-9M on order for F-16C/D.* Historically used on Lockheed F-104 Starfighter.
- Philippines - F-5 and F-8 Crusader
- Poland - AIM-9X
- Portugal
- Qatar - AIM-9M
- Saudi Arabia
- Singapore: Republic of Singapore Air Force - AIM-9J/P/S/X (Quantity: 400/264/96/200 missiles).
- South Africa - Used on the F-86 Sabre and Dassault Mirage III, replaced by IRIS-T and A-Darter.
- South Korea - used on McDonnell Douglas F-4 Phantom II, Northrop F-5, Boeing F-15E Strike Eagle, Lockheed F-16 Fighting Falcon families. Historically used on North American F-86 Sabre.
- Spain - AIM-9L, L(I) and JULI. Replaced by IRIS-T
- Sweden - *called Robot 24/24J (B and J equivalents) and Robot 74 (L equivalent), will be replaced by IRIS-T.*
- Switzerland
- Republic of China (Taiwan) - AIM-9P4: F-5E/F, F-CK-1 A/B/C/D, F-16A/B Block 20, AT-3A/B. AIM-9M/M-2: F-16A/B Block 20. Historically used on North American F-86 Sabre, Lockheed F-104 Starfighter, North American F-100 Super Sabre.
- Thailand use on JAS 39 C/D, F-16 A/B/ADF, F-5 E/F/T, L-39ZA/ART (Westernized weapon system), Alphajet.
- Turkey
- Tunisia AIM-9J
- United Kingdom - Being replaced by ASRAAM
- United States
- Venezuela, AIM-9B on VF-5 and Mirage 50 - AIM-9L on F-16A/B
- Zimbabwe

Please note that this list is not exhaustive.

Source http://en.wikipedia.org/wiki/AIM-9_Sidewinder

IRIS-T

1:1 model of the IRIS-T

Type	Short-range air-to-air missile
Place of origin	multinational with Germany as lead
Service history	
In service	December 2005
Used by	See *Users*
Production history	
Manufacturer	Diehl BGT Defence
Unit cost	€0.38m (~US$0.5m)
Specifications	
Weight	87.4 kg
Length	2936 mm
Diameter	127 mm
Warhead	HE/Fragmentation
Detonation mechanism	Impact and active radar proximity fuse
Engine	Solid-fuel rocket
Wingspan	447 mm
Operational range	~25 km
Flight altitude	Sea level to 20,000 m

Speed	Mach 3
Guidance system	Infrared
Launch platform	Users: ▬ Germany: Typhoon, Tornado, F-4 ▬ Greece: F-16, F-4 ▬ Italy: Typhoon ▬ Norway: F-16, NASAMS ▬ Sweden: Gripen ▬ Austria: Typhoon ▬ Spain: F-18, Typhoon ▬ South Africa: Gripen ▬ Saudi Arabia: Typhoon, Tornado ▬ Thailand: Gripen, F-16

The **IRIS-T (Infra Red Imaging System Tail/Thrust Vector-Controlled)** is a German-led program to develop a short-range air-to-air missile to replace the venerable AIM-9 Sidewinder found in some of the NATO member countries. Any aircraft capable of carrying and firing Sidewinder is also capable of launching IRIS-T.

History

Sorry, your browser either has JavaScript disabled or does not have any supported player.
You can download the clip or download a player to play the clip in your browser.
Movement of the seeker head

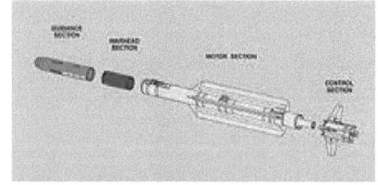

Subassemblies of the IRIS-T

In the 1980s, NATO countries signed a Memorandum of Agreement that the United States would develop a medium-

German Air Force soldiers mount an IRIS-T to an Eurofighter

range air-to-air missile to replace the AIM-7 Sparrow, while Britain and Germany would develop a short-range air-to-air missile to replace the AIM-9 Sidewinder. The US design developed as the AIM-120 AMRAAM, while the UK-German design developed as the AIM-132 ASRAAM.

The roots of the ASRAAM dated back to 1968 when development began on the Hawker Siddeley SRAAM ('Taildog'), but this project ended in 1974 with no production orders. This work was dusted off for the UK/German effort, with the Germans providing a new seeker, and the British providing most of the remaining components. In the intervening time, the need for high manoeuvrability was downgraded in favor of greater range.

As the AIM-120 worked at long ranges well in excess of 20 miles, the very short-range Sidewinders and original Taildog left a wide performance gap that needed to be filled. The original design was re-worked to produce a much less manoeuvrable design, removing the thrust vectoring, and thereby greatly improving speed and range.

After German reunification in 1990, Germany found itself with large stockpiles of the Soviet Vympel R-73 missiles (NATO reporting name: *AA-11 Archer*) carried by the MiG-29 Fulcrum and concluded that the AA-11's capabilities had been noticeably underestimated. In particular, it was found to be both far more manoeuvrable, and far more capable in terms of seeker acquisition and tracking than the latest AIM-9 Sidewinder. These conclusions led Germany to question certain aspects of the design of ASRAAM related to the airframe which was a British responsibility. Of particular concern was the lack of thrust vectoring to aid manoeuvrability in close-in air combat. When these concerns were raised, Germany and Britain could not come to an agreement about the design of ASRAAM, so in 1990 Germany withdrew from the ASRAAM project, while Britain resolved to find another seeker and develop ASRAAM according to the original requirements.

In late 1990, the US partnership expressed similar concerns and embarked on an upgrade to the existing Sidewinder design to provide increased manoeuvrability and IRCCM (infrared *counter* counter measures) performance, i.e. measures to counter infrared countermeasures (IRCM). This program was designated AIM-9X.

Missile characteristics

In comparison to the AIM-9L Sidewinder, the IRIS-T has higher ECM-resistance and flare suppression. Improvements in target discrimination not only allows for 5 to 8 times longer head-on firing range than the AIM9, it can also engage targets behind the launching aircraft, the latter made possible by the extreme close-in agility allowing turns of 60 g at a rate of 60°/s.

Development partners

In 1995, Germany announced the IRIS-T development program, in collaboration with Greece, Italy, Norway, Sweden and Canada. Canada later dropped out.

Workshare arrangements for IRIS-T development are:
Germany 46%
Italy 19%
Sweden 18%
Greece 13%
4% split between Canada and Norway.
In 2003 Spain joined as a partner for procurement.

The German Air Force took first delivery of the missile on 5 December 2005.

Variants

IDAS

The IDAS variant is a navalized version

of the missile, is also being developed for the new Type 212 submarine of the German Navy. IDAS is supposed to engage air threats, small or medium surface vessels or near land targets.

Model of IDAS

IRIS-T SL

Within the MEADS program, the German Air Force plans to integrate a land-launched radar-guided version of the missile, called IRIS-T SL. It has a pointed nose, unlike the normal IRIS-T.
IRIS-T SL missile
IRIS-T SL launch system

SAM Version

The Swedish Army plans to develop a ground launched version of the IRIS-T to replace the RBS 70 missile system.

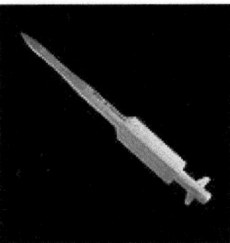

Users

 Germany
1,250

Spain
770 Original budget €247m, final cost €291m.

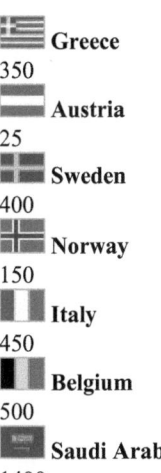

Greece
350

Austria
25

Sweden
400

Norway
150

Italy
450

Belgium
500

Saudi Arabia
1400

South Africa
10 (only 10 delivered out of an original order of 30)

Thailand
Delivered, unknown number to be ordered.
Source   http://en.wikipedia.org/wiki/IRIS-T

RBS-15

RBS-15

RBS-15 on right

Type	Fire-and-forget anti-ship and land attack
Place of origin	Sweden
Service history	
In service	1985- present
Used by	See *operators*
Production history	
Manufacturer	Saab Bofors Dynamics, Diehl BGT Defence
Specifications	
Weight	800 kg
Length	4.33 m
Diameter	50 cm
Warhead	200 kg HE blast and pre-fragmented
Detonation mechanism	impact or proximity
Engine	turbojet
Wingspan	1.4 m
Operational range	250 km
Flight altitude	sea skimming
Speed	subsonic
Guidance system	inertial, GPS, active radar (band)
Launch platform	naval ships, aircraft and lan based missile launchers

The **RBS-15** (Robotsystem 15) is a long-range fire-and-forget surface-to-surface and air-to-surface, anti-ship missile. The later version **Mk. III** has the ability to attack land targets as well. The missile was developed by the Swedish company Saab Bofors Dynamics.

History

The Swedish Navy was pioneering anti-ship missiles with the Halland Class of destroyers using the RB08 missile since the early 1960s. Owing to the Defence decision of 1958 the main effect for the navy was a restructuring into a lighter force consisting of FAC vessels and a halt to destroyer procurement. This posed a problem as the existing RB08 missile required launch rails and a missile magazine in the destroyers, taking up space that was simply not there on smaller ships. Adding to the problems, each missile had to be individually prepared for launch and only two missiles could be on the launch rails at the same time. In comparison, the STYX missile used by the Soviet Union (which was the expected adversary) stored the missiles in individual containers on deck which left the missiles immediately available for launch. Tests were carried out on Plejad class FACs with a single bow mounted RB08 in the late 1960s, but these tests came to nothing.

HMS Småland, radar and two RB 08 Missiles

RBS-15 Mk 1 on Swedish Missile Boat HMS Västervik

Next attempt by SAAB to take an order for anti-ship missiles to equip the Norrköping class FACs of the Swedish navy was first presented in 1978 as under the project name "RB 04 Turbo" a development of the air force RB 04E missile with a turbofan engine changed wing configurations and start rockets to take off from land. The initial proposal was rejected as inferior to the Harpoon. The project under the leadership of Hans Ahlinder then worked out a proposal for a missile with greater capabilities and superior performance to the Harpoon. As a way to indicate that it was a new weapon the project name was changed from "RB 04 Turbo" to "RBS-15"

RB04 Missile

The first weapon contract was signed in 1979, at the last minute the Swedish government had opted not to buy the Harpoon anti-ship missile and opting for an indigenous design. The first missiles were delivered to the Navy in June 1984, and the ship version **RBS-15 Mk. I** was introduced.

The missile had been ordered in 1984 by the Swedish Navy to develop a coastal defense version of the RBS-15F. The missile was taken into Swedish Navy service as the **Rb 15** by the Swedish Navy and became operational in 1985. The Swedish Air Force received their missiles a couple of years later. The Mk. I was produced from 1985 to 1990.

Work on a further developed version, the **RBS-15 Mk. II**, was initiated in the early 1980s. But it took until 1994, before a development contract was signed for the upgraded anti-ship missile. The Mk. II has the same range (70+ km), but the mid-course and terminal guidance system, as well as the radar and IR signature were upgraded. The Mk. II has been produced since 1998.

The development of the **RBS-15 Mk. III** began in the mid-1990s. Emphasis was put on increased range (due to larger fuel capacity and new fuel the range has been increased to some 200 km), improved accuracy (integrated GPS) and selectable priority targeting, which improved the weapon system's flexibility. The Mk. III missile will also be produced by Diehl BGT Defence of Germany for the new class of German stealth corvettes, and is likely to be later used on other German Navy vessels as well. Finnish truck maker Sisu produces missile launch trucks for RBS-15. The Mk. III has been in production since 2004.

Development phase

The missile was developed from the RB 04 missile that was used by the Swedish air force. The front of the missile was retained, including the warhead, but the rear received new wings and a turbofan engine replaced the rocket previously used. The RBS-15 underwent trials on the missile FAC HMS Piteå from 1983 and became operational with the Swedish Navy in 1985. The Västergötland class submarines were projected to have 4 vertical missile launch tubes for RBS-15 missiles in an extended hull but this was canceled due to budget constraints and it didn't fit the way Swedish submarines operated.

Versions

RBS-15 Mk. I
Powered by a French Microturbo TRI-60 engine, with a thrust of 3.73 kN (380 khp/830 lbf). Range 70+ km

RBS-15F
An Mk. I adapted for air launch. Entered service in 1989.

RBS-15 Mk. II
Range 70+ km. Designed to be launched from a number of different platforms, such as land-based launchers, aircraft, and ships.

RBS-15SF
Mk. II version for Finland. Local designation **MTO 85** (*Meritorjuntaohjus 1985*)

RBS-15 Mk. III
Range 200 km, with land attack capability. There is only a ship launched version. Production started in 2004. New Oval launch tubes instead of the old box type.

RBS-15SF-3
Both new Mk. IIIs and upgraded Mk. IIs, which have been upgraded to Mk. III standard. Finnish designation **MTO 85M**

RBS-15 Mk. IV
Currently being developed. Incorporates dual seekers, has a longer range and new missile link system. The radar signature has been reduced and its warhead can be changed depending on the mission. Future upgrades may include concept optimization for sea or land targets. The range of the Mk. IV would have to be significantly larger than others versions, over 1 000 km.

Operators

Current operators
 Croatia
It is the primary weapon of the Croatian Navy for its five guided missile corvettes and three coastal systems mounted on Tatra trucks. In total, 48

Croatian MOL with RBS-15 missiles

Croatian missile boat *Kralj Dmitar Zvonimir* with RBS-15 missiles

Mk.I units are in service but the serviceability of all missiles is questionable seen as only 28-30 are operational as of 2010. Plans for upgrading 21 missiles to the Mk.III standard was cancelled in 2009 due to budget restraints but light software upgrades are continuously executed and improve the missiles' navigation, precision and electronic defence. The latest of this upgrades was conducted in 2010 as a part of usual service works.

Finland

The Finnish Navy operates both RBS-15SF (Mk. IIs, designation **MTO 85**, 70 units) and RBS-15SF-3 (Mk. III, designation **MTO85M**, 48 units). The Mk. IIs are operated from *Rauma* class FACs (previously on *Helsinki* class vessels as well), and it is also mounted on Sisu trucks for mobile coastal defense. The Mk. IIIs are operated from *Hamina* class FACs. Older Mk. IIs (RBS-15F) have been upgraded to Mk. III standard (RBS-15K).

Germany

The German Navy has chosen the Mk. IIIs and Mk. IVs to equip its Braunschweig class corvettes and planned F125 class frigates and also plans to upgrade its Brandenburg class frigates with Mk. III

Poland

The Polish Navy has chosen the Mk. III to equip its Orkan class missile. A deal worth 110 million € was signed and the Orkan class ships modifications will be carried out by Thales Naval Netherlands. Mk.II missiles for Navy mobile land based launchers have also been delivered as part of the offset deal.

Sweden

The Swedish Navy operates the missiles from its *Stockholm*, *Göteborg* and *Visby* class corvettes. The Swedish coastal artillery was also equipped with RBS-15Ms, which were mounted on Volvo trucks. The Swedish Air Force operates the RBS-15F. The AJS 37 Viggen and the JAS 39 Gripen carries the missile, with the Viggen no longer in service . The following missiles are or have been used by the different branches: RB04E, RB08A, RBS08A, Mk. I, Mk. II Mk. III, RBS-15F), RBS-15K and RBS-15M.

On-order

Thailand

As a part of its Gripen procurement program, the Royal Thai Air Force will order the air-launch version, the RBS-15F, to equip its Gripen fighter aircraft in an agreement between Sweden and Thailand.

Former operators

Yugoslavia

Some RBS-15s were delivered during the late 80's for implementation on the new Yugoslavian Navy FACs to replace existing Russian-built missiles, but this project was never finalized due to the Yugoslav wars. Missiles have since ended up in the Croatian navy.

Source   http://en.wikipedia.org/wiki/RBS-15

RB 04

RB-04E

Type	Fire and forget anti-ship
Place of origin	Sweden

Service history

In service	1962-2000?
Used by	Sweden

Production history

Manufacturer	SAAB

Specifications

Weight	600kg (1,323lb)
Length	4.45m (14ft 7in)
Diameter	50cm (19.7in)
Warhead	300 kg (661 lb) HE blast ar pre-fragmented
Detonation mechanism	impact or proximity
Engine	INI Solid Rocket Engine
Wingspan	2.04m (6ft 8in)
Propellant	Solid
Operational range	32km (20 mi)
Flight altitude	sea skimming Rb04E
Speed	subsonic
Guidance system	active radar, Track on Jam (AGA-1 seeker, Rb04C)
Launch platform	Aircraft A 32, AJ 37, AJS ⁊

The **RB-04** (Robot 04) is a long-range fire-and-forget air-to-surface, anti-ship missile. The missile was known as the "RB-304" during development and early service years.

While interest in guided anti-ship missiles was subdued in the 1950s, it was not entirely extinct. In 1949, the Swedish government placed a request for a radar-guided, air-launched anti-ship missile. The request materialized as the SAAB "Robot-Byrån (RB) 04", which was first test launched by a Saab 29 Tunnan fighter in early 1955. The early versions of the missile suffered teething problems in regards to the two targeting modes, which were area attack, for striking a big group of ships (like an invasion fleet), and select targeting, where the missiles home in on a single vessel. In the area attack the missile would only target a ship in the group if they were within 1,000 meters of another vessel, this was also in the early electronic age, and changes in this distance required hardware modifications in a workshop.

RB-04C: The initial production version, the "RB-04C", entered service with Swedish Air Force A 32A Lansen attack aircraft in 1959. The RB-04C had a canard configuration, with short triangular cruciform fins around the nose, and two wide wings with fins attached to the wingtips. The RB-04C had a boost-sustain solid rocket motor and a SAP warhead that could be fitted with a contact or proximity fuse.

RB-04D: Further development of the C version. Longer range rocket engines and maintenance free thermal batteries where the main improoovements. Introduced in the late 1960s.

RB-04E: Further development of the D version to suit the new AJ37 Viggen strike aircraft. The missile had a shorter wingspan and improved guidance system and new monopulse radar seeker, which allowed sea-skimming approaches. This version was highly resistant to ECM and would automatically lock on especially powerful jamming signals.

Many components of the missile were reused when the RBS-15 was developed including the main body and warhead although the motor and main wings were the most obvious external changes.

The missile has never seen combat; the closest thing it has come to being

Robot 04 on A32A Lansen

used in anger was during the "Whiskey on the Rocks" incident when in 1981 a soviet (NATO code Whiskey Class) submarine ran aground outside the naval station in Karlskrona. Swedish AJ37 Viggens with Rb04E's slapped under their wings that had been taken from their top secret storage bunkers, stood on high alert for a possible soviet incursion to free their sub by force. On one occasion when a Soviet rescue operation seemed to be underway, aircraft were scrambled with the intent to intercept Soviet ships.

Source http://en.wikipedia.org/wiki/RB_04

Rb 05

Rb 05A	
Type	anti-ship, land attack and air-to-air
Service history	
In service	1967 - 2005
Production history	
Manufacturer	Saab-Scania, Missiles and Electronics
Specifications	
Weight	305 kg (672 lb)
Length	3.6 m (11.8 ft)
Diameter	0.3 m (11.8 in)
Warhead	160 kg high explosive
Engine	liquid propellant rocket motor
Wingspan	0.8 m (31.5 in)
Operational range	9 km (5.6 mi/4.9 nm)
Speed	supersonic
Guidance system	optical manual command
Launch platform	AJ 37 Viggen

The **Rb 05A** is a short-range air-to-surface missile that was developed in the 1960s by the Swedish company Saab-Scania, Missiles and Electronics.

History

The Rb 05A was developed as an air-to-surface missile for the AJ 37 Viggen in the late 1960s. The supersonic speed was deemed necessary to reduce the threat of surface-to-air missiles. The missile would usually be launched after a high-speed attack run on very low altitude and climb to 400m for launch. The aircraft would immediately descend again and the pilot guiding the missile optically with a joystick.

Guidance commands are transmitted via a microwave transmission link. Tracking flares on the missile aid the pilot in guiding the missile on target.

It was later discovered that the missile was effective in air-to-air against non-maneuvering aircraft as well.

A TV-guided variant Rb 05B was proposed to the Swedish Air Force in the early 1970s, but was turned down in favor of the AGM-65 Maverick/Rb 75 instead.

Operators

 Sweden

The Swedish Air Force operated the Rb 05A on the AJ 37 Viggen.

Similar missiles

AGM-12 Bullpup
AS-20
Kh-23

Source http://en.wikipedia.org/wiki/Rb_05

Skyflash

Prototype Panavia Tornado ADV aircraft wi semi-recessed Skyflash missiles

Type	Medium-range air-to-air missile
Place of origin	United Kingdom
Service history	
In service	1978-2006
Production history	
Manufacturer	British Aerospace Dynamic
Unit cost	£150,000 per round
Specifications	
Weight	193 kg (425 lb)
Length	3.68 m (12 ft 1 in)
Warhead	39.5 kg (87 lb)
Engine	Rocketdyne solid propellan rocket motor
Wingspan	1.02 m (3 ft 6 in)
Operational range	45 km (28 mi)
Speed	Mach 4
Guidance system	Marconi inverse monopulse semi-active radar homing

The British Aerospace **Skyflash** was a medium-range semi-active radar homing air-to-air missile derived from the US AIM-7 Sparrow missile and carried by Royal Air Force F-4 Phantoms and Tornado F3s, Italian Aeronautica Militare and Royal Saudi Air Force Tornados and Swedish Flygvapnet Viggens. The missile was replaced by the more capable AMRAAM.

History

Skyflash came out of a British plan to develop an inverse monopulse seeker for the Sparrow AIM-7E-2 by GEC and the RAE at the end of the 1960s. Having shown this was feasible Air Staff Requirement 1219 was issued in January 1972, with the project code XJ.521. The contractors were Hawker Siddeley and Marconi Space and Defence Systems (the renamed GEC guided weapons division). Major changes from the Sparrow were the addition of a Marconi semi-active inverse monopulse radar seeker, improved electronics, adapted control surfaces and a Thorn EMI active radar fuze. The rocket motors used were the Bristol Aerojet Mk 52 mod 2 and the Rocketdyne Mk 38 mod 4 rocket motor; the latest is the Aerojet Hoopoe.

Tests of the resulting missile showed it could function successfully in hostile Electronic Countermeasures (ECM) environments and could engage targets under a wide variety of conditions. It could be launched from as low as 100 m to attack a high-altitude target or launched at high level to engage a target flying as low as 75 m. The missile entered service on the F-4 Phantom II in 1978 as what was later called the 3000 Pre TEMP series (Tornado Embodied Modification Package).

In 1985, these aircraft were replaced with the Panavia Tornado ADV. Both the Phantom and the Tornado carry the Skyflash in semi-recessed wells on the aircraft's underbelly to reduce drag. In the Tornado, however, Frazer-Nash hydraulic trapezes project the missile out into the slipstream prior to motor ignition. This widens the missile's firing envelope by ensuring that the launch is not affected by turbulence from the fuselage. Skyflash was therefore converted to the 5000 TEMP series to incorporate the Fraser-Nash recesses in the body of the missile, Launch Attitude Control electronics in the autopilot section and improved wing surfaces. The Tornado-Skyflash combination became operational in 1987 with the formation of the first Tornado F.3 squadron.

From 1988 a further modification (6000 series) nicknamed "SuperTEMP" included the Hoopoe rocket motor to change the missile's flight profile from boost-and-glide (with a 4-second burn) to boost-sustain-glide (7-second burn), increasing its range and maneuverability.

In RAF service the missiles are usually carried in conjunction with four short-range air-to-air missiles, either AIM-9 Sidewinders or ASRAAMs.

A version with an active Thomson CSF-developed radar seeker and intertial mid-course update capability, Skyflash Mk 2 (called Active Skyflash), was proposed for both the RAF and Sweden. British interest ended with the 1981 Defence Review; BAe kept the proposal around until the early '90s but there were no buyers.

Further advanced Sky Flash derivatives were studied under the code name S225X, and these studies became the basis for the MBDA Meteor.

In 1996 the RAF announced the launch of the Capability Sustainment Programme which called for, among other things, the replacement of the Skyflash with the AIM-120 AMRAAM. AMRAAM incorporates an active seeker with a strapdown inertial reference unit and computer system, giving it fire-and-forget capability. The first Tornado ADV F.3 with limited AMRAAM capability entered service in 1998. In 2002, a further upgrade enabled full AMRAAM capability. The first mention of AMRAAM as a replacement for Skyflash dates back to 1986.

Characteristics

Primary function: Medium-range air-to-air missile
Main Contractor: BAe Dynamics, with Raytheon as subcontractor
Unit cost: £150,000 per round
Power Plant: Rocketdyne solid propellant rocket motor
Length: 3.68 m (12 ft 1 in)
Weight: 193 kg (425 lb)
Diameter: 0.203 m (8 in)
Wing span: 1.02 m (40 in)
Range: 45 km (28 mi)
Speed: Mach 4
Guidance system: Marconi inverse monopulse semi-active radar homing
Warheads: High explosive expanding ring with proximity fuse
Warhead weight: 39.5 kg (87 lb)

Users: UK (Royal Air Force), Saudi Arabia (Royal Saudi Air Force), Italy (on leased Tornado F3s), Sweden (Royal Swedish Air Force).
Date deployed: 1978
Date retired: Approx 2005-2006.

Former Operators

Italy
Italian Air Force

Saudi Arabia
Royal Saudi Air Force

Sweden
Royal Swedish Air force Made under license as the Robot 71

United Kingdom
Royal Air Force

Source http://en.wikipedia.org/wiki/Skyflash